Life Application Bible Studies
PHILIPPIANS & COLOSSIANS

APPLICATION® BIBLE STUDIES

philippians & colossians

Part 1:
Complete text of Philippians and Colossians with study notes and features from the *Life Application Study Bible*

Part 2:
Thirteen lessons for individual or group study

Study questions written and edited by

Peter O'Donnell
Rev. David R. Veerman
Dr. James C. Galvin
Dr. Bruce B. Barton

New Living Translation®

Tyndale House Publishers, Inc.
Carol Stream, Illinois

CONTENTS

A NOTE TO READERS

The *Holy Bible,* New Living Translation, was first published in 1996. It quickly became one of the most popular Bible translations in the English-speaking world. While the NLT's influence was rapidly growing, the Bible Translation Committee determined that an additional investment in scholarly review and text refinement could make it even better. So shortly after its initial publication, the committee began an eight-year process with the purpose of increasing the level of the NLT's precision without sacrificing its easy-to-understand quality. This second-generation text was completed in 2004 and is reflected in this edition of the New Living Translation. An additional update with minor changes was subsequently introduced in 2007.

The goal of any Bible translation is to convey the meaning and content of the ancient Hebrew, Aramaic, and Greek texts as accurately as possible to contemporary readers. The challenge for our translators was to create a text that would communicate as clearly and powerfully to today's readers as the original texts did to readers and listeners in the ancient biblical world. The resulting translation is easy to read and understand, while also accurately communicating the meaning and content of the original biblical texts. The NLT is a general-purpose text especially good for study, devotional reading, and reading aloud in worship services.

We believe that the New Living Translation—which combines the latest biblical scholarship with a clear, dynamic writing style—will communicate God's word powerfully to all who read it. We publish it with the prayer that God will use it to speak his timeless truth to the church and the world in a fresh, new way.

The Publishers
October 2007

INTRODUCTION TO THE
NEW LIVING TRANSLATION

Translation Philosophy and Methodology

English Bible translations tend to be governed by one of two general translation theories. The first theory has been called "formal-equivalence," "literal," or "word-for-word" translation. According to this theory, the translator attempts to render each word of the original language into English and seeks to preserve the original syntax and sentence structure as much as possible in translation. The second theory has been called "dynamic-equivalence," "functional-equivalence," or "thought-for-thought" translation. The goal of this translation theory is to produce in English the closest natural equivalent of the message expressed by the original-language text, both in meaning and in style.

Both of these translation theories have their strengths. A formal-equivalence translation preserves aspects of the original text—including ancient idioms, term consistency, and original-language syntax—that are valuable for scholars and professional study. It allows a reader to trace formal elements of the original-language text through the English translation. A dynamic-equivalence translation, on the other hand, focuses on translating the message of the original-language text. It ensures that the meaning of the text is readily apparent to the contemporary reader. This allows the message to come through with immediacy, without requiring the reader to struggle with foreign idioms and awkward syntax. It also facilitates serious study of the text's message and clarity in both devotional and public reading.

The pure application of either of these translation philosophies would create translations at opposite ends of the translation spectrum. But in reality, all translations contain a mixture of these two philosophies. A purely formal-equivalence translation would be unintelligible in English, and a purely dynamic-equivalence translation would risk being unfaithful to the original. That is why translations shaped by dynamic-equivalence theory are usually quite literal when the original text is relatively clear, and the translations shaped by formal-equivalence theory are sometimes quite dynamic when the original text is obscure.

The translators of the New Living Translation set out to render the message of the original texts of Scripture into clear, contemporary English. As they did so, they kept the concerns of both formal-equivalence and dynamic-equivalence in mind. On the one hand, they translated as simply and literally as possible when that approach yielded an accurate, clear, and natural English text. Many words and phrases were rendered literally and consistently into English, preserving essential literary and rhetorical devices, ancient metaphors, and word choices that give structure to the text and provide echoes of meaning from one passage to the next.

On the other hand, the translators rendered the message more dynamically when the literal rendering was hard to understand, was misleading, or yielded archaic or foreign wording. They clarified difficult metaphors and terms to aid in the reader's understanding. The translators first struggled with the meaning of the words and phrases in the ancient context; then they rendered the message into clear, natural English. Their goal was to be both faithful to the ancient texts and eminently readable. The result is a translation that is both exegetically accurate and idiomatically powerful.

Translation Process and Team

To produce an accurate translation of the Bible into contemporary English, the translation team needed the skills necessary to enter into the thought patterns of the ancient authors and then to render their ideas, connotations, and effects into clear, contemporary English.

To begin this process, qualified biblical scholars were needed to interpret the meaning of the original text and to check it against our base English translation. In order to guard against personal and theological biases, the scholars needed to represent a diverse group of evangelicals who would employ the best exegetical tools. Then to work alongside the scholars, skilled English stylists were needed to shape the text into clear, contemporary English.

With these concerns in mind, the Bible Translation Committee recruited teams of scholars that represented a broad spectrum of denominations, theological perspectives, and backgrounds within the worldwide evangelical community. Each book of the Bible was assigned to three different scholars with proven expertise in the book or group of books to be reviewed. Each of these scholars made a thorough review of a base translation and submitted suggested revisions to the appropriate Senior Translator. The Senior Translator then reviewed and summarized these suggestions and proposed a first-draft revision of the base text. This draft served as the basis for several additional phases of exegetical and stylistic committee review. Then the Bible Translation Committee jointly reviewed and approved every verse of the final translation.

Throughout the translation and editing process, the Senior Translators and their scholar teams were given a chance to review the editing done by the team of stylists. This ensured that exegetical errors would not be introduced late in the process and that the entire Bible Translation Committee was happy with the final result. By choosing a team of qualified scholars and skilled stylists and by setting up a process that allowed their interaction throughout the process, the New Living Translation has been refined to preserve the essential formal elements of the original biblical texts, while also creating a clear, understandable English text.

The New Living Translation was first published in 1996. Shortly after its initial publication, the Bible Translation Committee began a process of further committee review and translation refinement. The purpose of this continued revision was to increase the level of precision without sacrificing the text's easy-to-understand quality. This second-edition text was completed in 2004, and an additional update with minor changes was subsequently introduced in 2007. This printing of the New Living Translation reflects the updated 2007 text.

Written to Be Read Aloud

It is evident in Scripture that the biblical documents were written to be read aloud, often in public worship (see Nehemiah 8; Luke 4:16-20; 1 Timothy 4:13; Revelation 1:3). It is still the case today that more people will hear the Bible read aloud in church than are likely to read it for themselves. Therefore, a new translation must communicate with clarity and power when it is read publicly. Clarity was a primary goal for the NLT translators, not only to facilitate private reading and understanding, but also to ensure that it would be excellent for public reading and make an immediate and powerful impact on any listener.

The Texts behind the New Living Translation

The Old Testament translators used the Masoretic Text of the Hebrew Bible as represented in *Biblia Hebraica Stuttgartensia* (1977), with its extensive system of textual notes; this is an update of Rudolf Kittel's *Biblia Hebraica* (Stuttgart, 1937). The translators also further compared the Dead Sea Scrolls, the Septuagint and other Greek manuscripts, the Samaritan Pentateuch, the Syriac Peshitta, the Latin Vulgate, and any other versions or manuscripts that shed light on the meaning of difficult passages.

The New Testament translators used the two standard editions of the Greek New Testament: the *Greek New Testament*, published by the United Bible Societies (UBS, fourth revised edition, 1993), and *Novum Testamentum Graece*, edited by Nestle and Aland (NA, twenty-seventh edition, 1993). These two editions, which have the same text but differ in punctuation and textual notes, represent, for the most part, the best in modern textual scholarship. However, in cases where strong textual or other scholarly evidence supported the decision, the translators sometimes chose to differ from the UBS and NA Greek texts and followed variant readings found in other ancient witnesses. Significant textual variants of this sort are always noted in the textual notes of the New Living Translation.

Translation Issues

The translators have made a conscious effort to provide a text that can be easily understood by the typical reader of modern English. To this end, we sought to use only vocabulary and language structures in common use today. We avoided using language likely to become quickly dated or that reflects only a narrow subdialect of English, with the goal of making the New Living Translation as broadly useful and timeless as possible.

But our concern for readability goes beyond the concerns of vocabulary and sentence structure. We are also concerned about historical and cultural barriers to understanding the Bible, and we have sought to translate terms shrouded in history and culture in ways that can be immediately understood. To this end:

- We have converted ancient weights and measures (for example, "ephah" [a unit of dry volume] or "cubit" [a unit of length]) to modern English (American) equivalents, since the ancient measures are not generally meaningful to today's readers. Then in the textual footnotes we offer the literal Hebrew, Aramaic, or Greek measures, along with modern metric equivalents.

- Instead of translating ancient currency values literally, we have expressed them in common terms that communicate the message. For example, in the Old Testament, "ten shekels of silver" becomes "ten pieces of silver" to convey the intended message. In the New Testament, we have often translated the "denarius" as "the normal daily wage" to facilitate understanding. Then a footnote offers: "Greek *a denarius*, the payment for a full day's wage." In general, we give a clear English rendering and then state the literal Hebrew, Aramaic, or Greek in a textual footnote.

- Since the names of Hebrew months are unknown to most contemporary readers, and since the Hebrew lunar calendar fluctuates from year to year in relation to the solar calendar used today, we have looked for clear ways to communicate the time of year the Hebrew months (such as Abib) refer to. When an expanded or interpretive rendering is given in the text, a textual note gives the literal rendering. Where it is possible to define a specific ancient date in terms of our modern calendar, we use modern dates in the text. A textual footnote then gives the literal Hebrew date and states the rationale for our rendering. For example, Ezra 6:15 pinpoints the date when the postexilic Temple was completed in Jerusalem: "the third day of the month Adar." This was during the sixth year of King Darius's reign (that is, 515 B.C.). We have translated that date as March 12, with a footnote giving the Hebrew and identifying the year as 515 B.C.

- Since ancient references to the time of day differ from our modern methods of denoting time, we have used renderings that are instantly understandable to the modern reader. Accordingly, we have rendered specific times of day by using approximate equivalents in terms of our common "o'clock" system. On occasion, translations such as "at dawn the next morning" or "as the sun was setting" have been used when the biblical reference is more general.

- When the meaning of a proper name (or a wordplay inherent in a proper name) is relevant to the message of the text, its meaning is often illuminated with a textual footnote. For example, in Exodus 2:10 the text reads: "The princess named him Moses, for she explained, 'I lifted him out of the water.' " The accompanying footnote reads: "*Moses* sounds like a Hebrew term that means 'to lift out.' "

  Sometimes, when the actual meaning of a name is clear, that meaning is included in parentheses within the text itself. For example, the text at Genesis 16:11 reads: "You are to name him Ishmael (*which means 'God hears'*), for the LORD has heard your cry of distress." Since the original hearers and readers would have instantly understood the meaning of the name "Ishmael," we have provided modern readers with the same information so they can experience the text in a similar way.

- Many words and phrases carry a great deal of cultural meaning that was obvious to the original readers but needs explanation in our own culture. For example, the phrase "they beat their breasts" (Luke 23:48) in ancient times meant that people were very upset, often in mourning. In our translation we chose to translate this phrase dynamically for clarity: "They went home *in deep sorrow*." Then we included a footnote with the literal Greek, which reads: "Greek *went home beating their breasts*." In other similar cases, however, we have sometimes chosen to illuminate the existing literal expression to make it immediately understandable. For example, here we might have expanded the literal Greek phrase to read: "They went home beating their breasts *in sorrow.*" If we had done this, we would not have included a textual footnote, since the literal Greek clearly appears in translation.

- Metaphorical language is sometimes difficult for contemporary readers to understand, so at times we have chosen to translate or illuminate the meaning of a metaphor. For example, the ancient poet writes, "Your neck is *like* the tower of David" (Song of Songs 4:4). We have rendered it "Your neck is *as beautiful as* the tower of David" to clarify the intended positive meaning of the simile. Another example comes in Ecclesiastes 12:3, which can be literally rendered: "Remember him . . . when the grinding women cease because they are few, and the women who look through the windows see dimly." We have rendered it: "Remember him before your teeth—your few remaining servants—stop grinding; and before your eyes—the women looking through the windows—see dimly." We clarified such metaphors only when we believed a typical reader might be confused by the literal text.

- When the content of the original language text is poetic in character, we have rendered it in English poetic form. We sought to break lines in ways that clarify and highlight the relationships between phrases of the text. Hebrew poetry often uses parallelism, a literary form where a second phrase (or in some instances a third or fourth) echoes the initial phrase in some way. In Hebrew parallelism, the subsequent parallel phrases continue, while also furthering and sharpening, the thought expressed in the initial line or phrase. Whenever possible, we sought to represent these parallel phrases in natural poetic English.

- The Greek term *hoi Ioudaioi* is literally translated "the Jews" in many English translations. In the Gospel of John, however, this term doesn't always refer to the Jewish people generally. In some contexts, it refers more particularly to the Jewish religious leaders. We have attempted to capture the meaning in these different contexts by using terms such as "the people" (with a footnote: Greek *the Jewish people*) or "the religious leaders," where appropriate.

- One challenge we faced was how to translate accurately the ancient biblical text that was originally written in a context where male-oriented terms were used to refer to humanity generally. We needed to respect the nature of the ancient context while also trying to make the translation clear to a modern audience that tends to read male-oriented language as applying only to males. Often the original text, though using masculine nouns and pronouns, clearly intends that the message be applied to both men and women. A typical example is found in the New Testament letters, where the believers are called "brothers" (*adelphoi*). Yet it is clear from the content of these letters that they were addressed to all the believers—male and female. Thus, we have usually translated this Greek word as "brothers and sisters" in order to represent the historical situation more accurately.

  We have also been sensitive to passages where the text applies generally to human beings or to the human condition. In some instances we have used plural pronouns (they, them) in place of the masculine singular (he, him). For example, a traditional rendering of Proverbs 22:6 is: "Train up a child in the way he should go, and when he is old he will not turn from it." We have rendered it: "Direct your children onto the right path, and when they are older, they will not leave it." At times, we have also replaced third person pronouns with the second person to ensure clarity. A traditional rendering of Proverbs 26:27 is: "He who digs a pit will fall into it, and he who rolls a stone, it will come back on him." We have rendered it: "If you set a trap for others, you will get caught in it yourself. If you roll a boulder down on others, it will crush you instead."

  We should emphasize, however, that all masculine nouns and pronouns used to represent God (for example, "Father") have been maintained without exception. All decisions of this kind have been driven by the concern to reflect accurately the intended meaning of the original texts of Scripture.

Lexical Consistency in Terminology
For the sake of clarity, we have translated certain original-language terms consistently, especially within synoptic passages and for commonly repeated rhetorical phrases, and within

certain word categories such as divine names and non-theological technical terminology (e.g., liturgical, legal, cultural, zoological, and botanical terms). For theological terms, we have allowed a greater semantic range of acceptable English words or phrases for a single Hebrew or Greek word. We have avoided some theological terms that are not readily understood by many modern readers. For example, we avoided using words such as "justification" and "sanctification," which are carryovers from Latin translations. In place of these words, we have provided renderings such as "made right with God" and "made holy."

The Spelling of Proper Names

Many individuals in the Bible, especially the Old Testament, are known by more than one name (e.g., Uzziah/Azariah). For the sake of clarity, we have tried to use a single spelling for any one individual, footnoting the literal spelling whenever we differ from it. This is especially helpful in delineating the kings of Israel and Judah. King Joash/Jehoash of Israel has been consistently called Jehoash, while King Joash/Jehoash of Judah is called Joash. A similar distinction has been used to distinguish between Joram/Jehoram of Israel and Joram/Jehoram of Judah. All such decisions were made with the goal of clarifying the text for the reader. When the ancient biblical writers clearly had a theological purpose in their choice of a variant name (e.g., Esh-baal/Ishbosheth), the different names have been maintained with an explanatory footnote.

For the names Jacob and Israel, which are used interchangeably for both the individual patriarch and the nation, we generally render it "Israel" when it refers to the nation and "Jacob" when it refers to the individual. When our rendering of the name differs from the underlying Hebrew text, we provide a textual footnote, which includes this explanation: "The names 'Jacob' and 'Israel' are often interchanged throughout the Old Testament, referring sometimes to the individual patriarch and sometimes to the nation."

The Rendering of Divine Names

All appearances of *'el, 'elohim,* or *'eloah* have been translated "God," except where the context demands the translation "god(s)." We have generally rendered the tetragrammaton (*YHWH*) consistently as "the Lord," utilizing a form with small capitals that is common among English translations. This will distinguish it from the name *'adonai,* which we render "Lord." When *'adonai* and *YHWH* appear together, we have rendered it "Sovereign Lord." This also distinguishes *'adonai YHWH* from cases where *YHWH* appears with *'elohim,* which is rendered "Lord God." When *YH* (the short form of *YHWH*) and *YHWH* appear together, we have rendered it "Lord God." When *YHWH* appears with the term *tseba'oth,* we have rendered it "Lord of Heaven's Armies" to translate the meaning of the name. In a few cases, we have utilized the transliteration, *Yahweh,* when the personal character of the name is being invoked in contrast to another divine name or the name of some other god (for example, see Exodus 3:15; 6:2-3).

In the New Testament, the Greek word *christos* has been translated as "Messiah" when the context assumes a Jewish audience. When a Gentile audience can be assumed, *christos* has been translated as "Christ." The Greek word *kurios* is consistently translated "Lord," except that it is translated "Lord" wherever the New Testament text explicitly quotes from the Old Testament, and the text there has it in small capitals.

Textual Footnotes

The New Living Translation provides several kinds of textual footnotes, all designated in the text with an asterisk:

- When for the sake of clarity the NLT renders a difficult or potentially confusing phrase dynamically, we generally give the literal rendering in a textual footnote. This allows the reader to see the literal source of our dynamic rendering and how our translation relates to other more literal translations. These notes are prefaced with "Hebrew," "Aramaic," or "Greek," identifying the language of the underlying source text. For example, in Acts 2:42 we translated the literal "breaking of bread" (from the Greek) as "the Lord's Supper" to clarify that this verse refers to the ceremonial practice of the church rather than just an ordinary meal. Then we attached a footnote to "the Lord's Supper," which reads: "Greek *the breaking of bread.*"

- Textual footnotes are also used to show alternative renderings, prefaced with the word "Or." These normally occur for passages where an aspect of the meaning is debated. On occasion, we also provide notes on words or phrases that represent a departure from long-standing tradition. These notes are prefaced with "Tradition-ally rendered." For example, the footnote to the translation "serious skin disease" at Leviticus 13:2 says: "Traditionally rendered *leprosy*. The Hebrew word used throughout this passage is used to describe various skin diseases."
- When our translators follow a textual variant that differs significantly from our stan-dard Hebrew or Greek texts (listed earlier), we document that difference with a foot-note. We also footnote cases when the NLT excludes a passage that is included in the Greek text known as the *Textus Receptus* (and familiar to readers through its transla-tion in the King James Version). In such cases, we offer a translation of the excluded text in a footnote, even though it is generally recognized as a later addition to the Greek text and not part of the original Greek New Testament.
- All Old Testament passages that are quoted in the New Testament are identified by a textual footnote at the New Testament location. When the New Testament clearly quotes from the Greek translation of the Old Testament, and when it differs signifi-cantly in wording from the Hebrew text, we also place a textual footnote at the Old Testament location. This note includes a rendering of the Greek version, along with a cross-reference to the New Testament passage(s) where it is cited (for example, see notes on Proverbs 3:12; Psalms 8:2; 53:3).
- Some textual footnotes provide cultural and historical information on places, things, and people in the Bible that are probably obscure to modern readers. Such notes should aid the reader in understanding the message of the text. For example, in Acts 12:1, "King Herod" is named in this translation as "King Herod Agrippa" and is iden-tified in a footnote as being "the nephew of Herod Antipas and a grandson of Herod the Great."
- When the meaning of a proper name (or a wordplay inherent in a proper name) is relevant to the meaning of the text, it is either illuminated with a textual footnote or included within parentheses in the text itself. For example, the footnote concerning the name "Eve" at Genesis 3:20 reads: "*Eve* sounds like a Hebrew term that means 'to give life.'" This wordplay in the Hebrew illuminates the meaning of the text, which goes on to say that Eve "would be the mother of all who live."

As WE SUBMIT this translation for publication, we recognize that any translation of the Scrip-tures is subject to limitations and imperfections. Anyone who has attempted to communi-cate the richness of God's Word into another language will realize it is impossible to make a perfect translation. Recognizing these limitations, we sought God's guidance and wisdom throughout this project. Now we pray that he will accept our efforts and use this translation for the benefit of the church and of all people.

We pray that the New Living Translation will overcome some of the barriers of history, cul-ture, and language that have kept people from reading and understanding God's Word. We hope that readers unfamiliar with the Bible will find the words clear and easy to understand and that readers well versed in the Scriptures will gain a fresh perspective. We pray that readers will gain insight and wisdom for living, but most of all that they will meet the God of the Bible and be forever changed by knowing him.

The Bible Translation Committee
October 2007

WHY THE
LIFE APPLICATION STUDY BIBLE
IS UNIQUE

Have you ever opened your Bible and asked the following:

- What does this passage really mean?
- How does it apply to my life?
- Why does some of the Bible seem irrelevant?
- What do these ancient cultures have to do with today?
- I love God; why can't I understand what he is saying to me through his word?
- What's going on in the lives of these Bible people?

Many Christians do not read the Bible regularly. Why? Because in the pressures of daily living they cannot find a connection between the timeless principles of Scripture and the ever-present problems of day-by-day living.

God urges us to apply his word (Isaiah 42:23; 1 Corinthians 10:11; 2 Thessalonians 3:4), but too often we stop at accumulating Bible knowledge. This is why the *Life Application Study Bible* was developed—to show how to put into practice what we have learned.

Applying God's word is a vital part of one's relationship with God; it is the evidence that we are obeying him. The difficulty in applying the Bible is not with the Bible itself, but with the reader's inability to bridge the gap between the past and present, the conceptual and practical. When we don't or can't do this, spiritual dryness, shallowness, and indifference are the results.

The words of Scripture itself cry out to us, "But don't just listen to God's word. You must do what it says. Otherwise, you are only fooling yourselves" (James 1:22). The *Life Application Study Bible* helps us to obey God's word. Developed by an interdenominational team of pastors, scholars, family counselors, and a national organization dedicated to promoting God's word and spreading the gospel, the *Life Application Study Bible* took many years to complete. All the work was reviewed by several renowned theologians under the directorship of Dr. Kenneth Kantzer.

The *Life Application Study Bible* does what a good resource Bible should: It helps you understand the context of a passage, gives important background and historical information, explains difficult words and phrases, and helps you see the interrelationship of Scripture. But it does much more. The *Life Application Study Bible* goes deeper into God's word, helping you discover the timeless truth being communicated, see the relevance for your life, and make a personal application. While some study Bibles attempt application, over 75 percent of this Bible is application oriented. The notes answer the questions "So what?" and "What does this passage mean to me, my family, my friends, my job, my neighborhood, my church, my country?"

Imagine reading a familiar passage of Scripture and gaining fresh insight, as if it were the first time you had ever read it. How much richer your life would be if you left each Bible reading with a new perspective and a small change for the better. A small change every day adds up to a changed life—and that is the very purpose of Scripture.

WHAT IS APPLICATION?

The best way to define application is to first determine what it is *not*. Application is *not* just accumulating knowledge. Accumulating knowledge helps us discover and understand facts and concepts, but it stops there. History is filled with philosophers who knew what the Bible said but failed to apply it to their lives, keeping them from believing and changing. Many think that understanding is the end goal of Bible study, but it is really only the beginning.

Application is *not* just illustration. Illustration only tells us how someone else handled a similar situation. While we may empathize with that person, we still have little direction for our personal situation.

Application is *not* just making a passage "relevant." Making the Bible relevant only helps us to see that the same lessons that were true in Bible times are true today; it does not show us how to apply them to the problems and pressures of our individual lives.

What, then, is application? Application begins by knowing and understanding God's word and its timeless truths. *But you cannot stop there*. If you do, God's word may not change your life, and it may become dull, difficult, tedious, and tiring. A good application focuses the truth of God's word, shows the reader what to do about what is being read, and motivates the reader to respond to what God is teaching. All three are essential to application.

Application is putting into practice what we already know (see Mark 4:24 and Hebrews 5:14) and answering the question "So what?" by confronting us with the right questions and motivating us to take action (see 1 John 2:5-6 and James 2:26). Application is deeply personal—unique for each individual. It makes a relevant truth a personal truth and involves developing a strategy and action plan to live your life in harmony with the Bible. It is the biblical "how to" of life.

You may ask, "How can your application notes be relevant to my life?" Each application note has three parts: (1) an *explanation*, which ties the note directly to the Scripture passage and sets up the truth that is being taught; (2) the *bridge*, which explains the timeless truth and makes it relevant for today; (3) the *application*, which shows you how to take the timeless truth and apply it to your personal situation. No note, by itself, can apply Scripture directly to your life. It can only teach, direct, lead, guide, inspire, recommend, and urge. It can give you the resources and direction you need to apply the Bible, but only you can take these resources and put them into practice.

A good note, therefore should not only give you knowledge and understanding but point you to application. Before you buy any kind of resource study Bible, you should evaluate the notes and ask the following questions: (1) Does the note contain enough information to help me understand the point of the Scripture passage? (2) Does the note assume I know more than I do? (3) Does the note avoid denominational bias? (4) Do the notes touch most of life's experiences? (5) Does the note help me apply God's word?

FEATURES OF THE
LIFE APPLICATION STUDY BIBLE

NOTES

In addition to providing the reader with many application notes, the *Life Application Study Bible* also offers several kinds of explanatory notes, which help the reader understand culture, history, context, difficult-to-understand passages, background, places, theological concepts, and the relationship of various passages in Scripture to other passages.

BOOK INTRODUCTIONS

Each book introduction is divided into several easy-to-find parts:

Timeline. A guide that puts the Bible book into its historical setting. It lists the key events and the dates when they occurred.

Vital Statistics. A list of straight facts about the book—those pieces of information you need to know at a glance.

Overview. A summary of the book with general lessons and applications that can be learned from the book as a whole.

Blueprint. The outline of the book. It is printed in easy-to-understand language and is designed for easy memorization. To the right of each main heading is a key lesson that is taught in that particular section.

Megathemes. A section that gives the main themes of the Bible book, explains their significance, and then tells you why they are still important for us today.

Map. If included, this shows the key places found in that book and retells the story of the book from a geographical point of view.

OUTLINE

The *Life Application Study Bible* has a new, custom-made outline that was designed specifically from an application point of view. Several unique features should be noted:

1. To avoid confusion and to aid memory work, the book outline has only three levels for headings. Main outline heads are marked with a capital letter. Subheads are marked by a number. Minor explanatory heads have no letter or number.

2. Each main outline head marked by a letter also has a brief paragraph below it summarizing the Bible text and offering a general application.

3. Parallel passages are listed where they apply.

PERSONALITY PROFILES

Among the unique features of this Bible are the profiles of key Bible people, including their strengths and weaknesses, greatest accomplishments and mistakes, and key lessons from their lives.

MAPS

The *Life Application Study Bible* has a thorough and comprehensive Bible atlas built right into the book. There are two kinds of maps: a book-introduction map, telling the story of the book, and thumbnail maps in the notes, plotting most geographic movements.

CHARTS AND DIAGRAMS

Many charts and diagrams are included to help the reader better visualize difficult concepts or relationships. Most charts not only present the needed information but show the significance of the information as well.

CROSS-REFERENCES

An updated, exhaustive cross-reference system in the margins of the Bible text helps the reader find related passages quickly.

TEXTUAL NOTES

Directly related to the text of the New Living Translation, the textual notes provide explanations on certain wording in the translation, alternate translations, and information about readings in the ancient manuscripts.

HIGHLIGHTED NOTES

In each Bible study lesson, you will be asked to read specific notes as part of your preparation. These notes have each been highlighted by a bullet (•) so that you can find them easily.

PHILIPPIANS

VITAL STATISTICS

PURPOSE:
To thank the Philippians for the gift they had sent Paul and to strengthen these believers by showing them that true joy comes from Jesus Christ alone

AUTHOR:
Paul

ORIGINAL AUDIENCE:
The Christians at Philippi

DATE WRITTEN:
Approximately A.D. 61, from Rome during Paul's imprisonment there

SETTING:
Paul and his companions began the church at Philippi on his second missionary journey (Acts 16:11–40). This was the first church established on the European continent. The Philippian church had sent a gift with Epaphroditus (one of their members) to be delivered to Paul (4:18). Paul was in a Roman prison at the time. He wrote this letter to thank them for their gift and to encourage them in their faith.

KEY VERSE:
"Always be full of joy in the Lord. I say it again—rejoice!" (4:4)

KEY PEOPLE:
Paul, Timothy, Epaphroditus, Euodia, and Syntyche

KEY PLACE:
Philippi

THE WORD *happiness* evokes visions of unwrapping gifts on Christmas morning, strolling hand in hand with the one you love, being surprised on your birthday, responding with unbridled laughter to a comedian, or vacationing in an exotic locale. Everyone wants to be happy; we make chasing this elusive ideal a lifelong pursuit: spending money, collecting things, and searching for new experiences. But if happiness depends on our circumstances, what happens when the toys rust, loved ones die, health deteriorates, money is stolen, and the party's over? Often happiness flees and despair sets in.

In contrast to *happiness* stands *joy.* Running deeper and stronger, joy is the quiet, confident assurance of God's love and work in our lives—that he will be there no matter what! Happiness depends on happenings, but joy depends on Christ.

Philippians is Paul's joy letter. The church in that Macedonian city had been a great encouragement to Paul. The Philippian believers had enjoyed a very special relationship with him, so he wrote them a personal expression of his love and affection. They had brought him great joy (4:1). Philippians is also a joyful book because it emphasizes the real joy of the Christian life. The concept of *rejoicing* or *joy* appears sixteen times in four chapters, and the pages radiate this positive message, culminating in the exhortation to "always be full of joy in the Lord. I say it again—rejoice!" (4:4).

In a life dedicated to serving Christ, Paul had faced excruciating poverty, abundant wealth, and everything in between. He even wrote this joyful letter from prison. Whatever the circumstances, Paul had learned to be content (4:11, 12), finding real joy as he focused all of his attention and energy on knowing Christ (3:8) and obeying him (3:12, 13).

Paul's desire to know Christ above all else is wonderfully expressed in the following words: "Yes, everything else is worthless when compared with the infinite value of knowing Christ Jesus my Lord. For his sake I have discarded everything else, counting it all as garbage, so that I could gain Christ and become one with him. . . . I want to know Christ and experience the mighty power that raised him from the dead. I want to suffer with him, sharing in his death" (3:8–10). May we share Paul's aspiration and seek to know Jesus Christ more and more. Rejoice with Paul in Philippians, and rededicate yourself to finding joy in Christ.

THE BLUEPRINT

1. Joy in suffering (1:1–30)
2. Joy in serving (2:1–30)
3. Joy in believing (3:1—4:1)
4. Joy in giving (4:2–23)

Although Paul was writing from prison, joy is a dominant theme in this letter. The secret of his joy is grounded in his relationship with Christ. People today desperately want to be happy but are tossed and turned by daily successes, failures, and inconveniences. Christians are to be joyful in every circumstance, even when things are going badly, even when we feel like complaining, even when no one else is joyful. Christ still reigns, and we still know him, so we can rejoice at all times.

MEGATHEMES

THEME	EXPLANATION	IMPORTANCE
Humility	Christ showed true humility when he laid aside his rights and privileges as God to become human. He poured out his life to pay the penalty we deserve. Laying aside self-interest is essential to all our relationships.	We are to take Christ's attitude in serving others. We must renounce personal recognition and merit. When we give up our self-interest, we can serve with joy, love, and kindness.
Self-Sacrifice	Christ suffered and died so we might have eternal life. With courage and faithfulness, Paul sacrificed himself for the ministry. He preached the gospel even while he was in prison.	Christ gives us power to lay aside our personal needs and concerns. To utilize his power, we must imitate those leaders who show self-denying concern for others. We dare not be self-centered.
Unity	In every church, in every generation, there are divisive influences (issues, loyalties, and conflicts). In the midst of hardships, it is easy to turn on one another. Paul encouraged the Philippians to agree with one another, stop complaining, and work together.	As believers, we should not contend with one another but unite against a mutual enemy. When we are unified in love, Christ's strength is most abundant. Keep before you the ideals of teamwork, consideration of others, and unselfishness.
Christian Living	Paul shows us how to live successful Christian lives. We can become mature by being so identified with Christ that his attitude of humility and self-sacrifice becomes ours. Christ is both our source of power and our guide.	Developing our character begins with God's work in us. But growth also requires self-discipline, obedience to God's Word, and concentration on our part.
Joy	Believers can have profound contentment, serenity, and peace no matter what happens. This joy comes from knowing Christ personally and from depending on his strength rather than our own.	We can have joy, even in hardship. Joy does not come from outward circumstances but from inward strength. As Christians, we must not rely on what we have or what we experience to give us joy but on Christ within us.

1. Joy in suffering
Greetings from Paul

1:1
Acts 16:1
2 Cor 1:1

1 This letter is from Paul and Timothy, slaves of Christ Jesus.

I am writing to all of God's holy people in Philippi who belong to Christ Jesus, including the elders* and deacons.

1:2-3
Rom 1:7-8

²May God our Father and the Lord Jesus Christ give you grace and peace.

1:1 Or *overseers;* or *bishops.*

• **1:1** This is a personal letter to the Philippians, not intended for general circulation to all the churches, as was the letter to the Ephesians. Paul wanted to thank the believers for helping him when he had a need. He also wanted to tell them why he could be full of joy despite his imprisonment and upcoming trial. In this uplifting letter, Paul counseled the Philippians about humility and unity and warned them about potential problems.

• **1:1** On Paul's first missionary journey, he visited towns close to his headquarters in Antioch of Syria. On his second and third journeys, he traveled farther away. Because of the great distances between the congregations that Paul had founded, he could no longer personally oversee them all. Thus, he was compelled to write letters to teach and encourage the believers. Fortunately, Paul had a staff of volunteers (including Timothy, Mark, and Epaphras) who personally delivered these letters and often remained with the congregations for a while to teach and encourage them.

• **1:1** For more information on Paul, see his Profile in Acts 9, p. 1837. Timothy's Profile is found in 1 Timothy 2, p. 2059.

• **1:1** The Roman colony of Philippi was located in northern Greece (called Macedonia in Paul's day). Philip II of Macedon (the father of Alexander the Great) took the town from ancient Thrace in about 357 B.C., enlarged and strengthened it, and gave it his name. This thriving commercial center sat at the crossroads between Europe and Asia. In about A.D. 50, Paul, Silas, Timothy, and Luke crossed the Aegean Sea from Asia Minor and landed at Philippi (Acts 16:11-40). The church in Philippi consisted mostly of Gentile (non-Jewish) believers. Because they were not familiar with the Old Testament, Paul did not specifically quote any Old Testament passages in this letter.

• **1:1** Elders (bishops or pastors) and deacons led the early Christian churches. The qualifications and duties of the elders are explained in detail in 1 Timothy 3:1-7 and Titus 1:5-9. The qualifications and duties of deacons are spelled out in 1 Timothy 3:8-13.

1:2 We get upset at children who fail to appreciate small gifts, yet we undervalue God's immeasurable gifts of grace and peace. Instead, we seek the possessions and shallow experiences the

Paul's Thanksgiving and Prayer

³Every time I think of you, I give thanks to my God. ⁴Whenever I pray, I make my requests for all of you with joy, ⁵for you have been my partners in spreading the Good News about Christ from the time you first heard it until now. ⁶And I am certain that God, who began the good work within you, will continue his work until it is finally finished on the day when Christ Jesus returns.

1:6 1 Cor 1:8

⁷So it is right that I should feel as I do about all of you, for you have a special place in my heart. You share with me the special favor of God, both in my imprisonment and in defending and confirming the truth of the Good News. ⁸God knows how much I love you and long for you with the tender compassion of Christ Jesus.

1:7 2 Cor 7:3

1:8 Rom 1:9

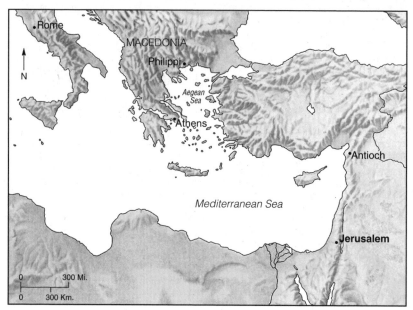

LOCATION OF PHILIPPI
Philippi sat on the Egnatian Way, the main transportation route in Macedonia, an extension of the Appian Way, which joined the eastern empire with Italy.

world offers. Compared to the big and bright "packages" of our culture, grace and peace appear insignificant. But when we unwrap them, we discover God's wonderful personal dealings with us. Inside the tiny package marked "grace and peace," we find an inexhaustible treasure of God's daily presence in our lives. Using these two words in his greetings to all the churches to whom he wrote, Paul wasn't offering something new. He was reminding his readers of what they already possessed in Christ. Thank God for his grace, and live in his peace.

● **1:4** This is the first of many times Paul used the word *joy* in this letter. The Philippians were remembered with joy and thanksgiving whenever Paul prayed. By helping Paul, they were helping Christ's cause. The Philippians were willing to be used by God for whatever he wanted them to do. When others think about you, what comes to their minds? Are you remembered with joy by them? Do your acts of kindness lift up others?

● **1:4, 5** The Philippians first heard the Good News about 10 years earlier when Paul and his companions visited Philippi (during Paul's second missionary journey) and founded the church there.

1:5 When Paul said that the Philippians were partners in spreading the Good News, he was remembering how they contributed through their practical help when Paul was in Philippi and through their financial support when he was in prison. As we help our ministers, missionaries, and evangelists through prayer, hospitality, and financial gifts, we become partners with them in spreading the gospel message.

● **1:6** The God who began a good work within us continues it throughout our lifetime and will finish it when we meet him face to face. God's work *for* us began when Christ died on the cross in our place. His work *within* us began when we first believed. Now the Holy Spirit lives in us, enabling us to be more like Christ every day. Paul is describing the process of Christian growth and maturity that began when we accepted Jesus and continues until Christ returns.

● **1:6** Do you sometimes feel as though you aren't making progress in your spiritual life? When God starts a project, he completes it! As with the Philippians, God will help you grow in grace until he has completed his work in your life. When you are discouraged, remember that God won't give up on you. He promises to finish the work he has begun. When you feel incomplete, unfinished, or distressed by your shortcomings, remember God's promise and provision. Don't let your present condition rob you of the joy of knowing Christ or keep you from growing closer to him.

● **1:7** When he mentions his imprisonment, Paul was probably referring to his imprisonment in Philippi (see Acts 16:22-36). In verses 13 and 14, Paul speaks of his Roman imprisonment. Wherever Paul was, even in prison, he faithfully preached the Good News. Remember Paul's inspiring example when hindrances, small or large, slow down your work for God.

● **1:7, 8** Have you ever longed to see a friend with whom you share fond memories? Paul had such a longing to see the Christians at Philippi. His love and affection for them was based not

1:9
1 Thes 3:12

1:10
Rom 12:2
1 Cor 1:8

1:11
John 15:4

9I pray that your love will overflow more and more, and that you will keep on growing in knowledge and understanding. 10For I want you to understand what really matters, so that you may live pure and blameless lives until the day of Christ's return. 11May you always be filled with the fruit of your salvation—the righteous character produced in your life by Jesus Christ*—for this will bring much glory and praise to God.

Paul's Joy That Christ Is Preached

1:12
2 Tim 2:9

1:13
Acts 28:30-31
Eph 3:1; 4:1

1:14
Phil 1:20

1:15
Phil 2:3

1:17
Acts 21:33

12And I want you to know, my dear brothers and sisters,* that everything that has happened to me here has helped to spread the Good News. 13For everyone here, including the whole palace guard,* knows that I am in chains because of Christ. 14And because of my imprisonment, most of the believers* here have gained confidence and boldly speak God's message* without fear.

15It's true that some are preaching out of jealousy and rivalry. But others preach about Christ with pure motives. 16They preach because they love me, for they know I have been appointed to defend the Good News. 17Those others do not have pure motives as they preach about Christ. They preach with selfish ambition, not sincerely, intending to make my chains more painful to me. 18But that doesn't matter. Whether their motives are false or

1:11 Greek *with the fruit of righteousness through Jesus Christ.*   **1:12** Greek *brothers.*   **1:13** Greek *including all the Praetorium.*   **1:14a** Greek *brothers in the Lord.*   **1:14b** Some manuscripts read *speak the message.*

---

merely on past experiences but also on the unity that comes when believers draw upon Christ's love. All Christians are part of God's family and thus share equally in the transforming power of his love. Do you feel a deep love for fellow Christians, friends and strangers alike? Let Christ's love motivate you to love other Christians and to express that love in your actions toward them.

1:9 Often the best way to influence someone is to pray for him or her. Paul's prayer for the Philippians was that they would be unified in love. Their love was to result in greater knowledge of Christ and deeper understanding (moral discernment). Their love was not based on feelings but on what Christ had done for them. As you grow in Christ's love, your heart and mind must grow together. Are your love and insight growing?

● **1:10** Paul prayed that the Philippian believers would have the ability to differentiate between right and wrong, good and bad, vital and trivial. We ought to pray for moral discernment so we can maintain our Christian morals and values. Hebrews 5:14 emphasizes the need for discernment.

1:10 "The day of Christ's return" refers to the time when God will judge the world through Jesus Christ. We should live each day as though he might return at any moment.

1:11 The "fruit of your salvation" includes all of the character traits flowing from a right relationship with God. There is no other way for us to gain this fruit of righteousness than through Christ. See Galatians 5:22, 23 for the "fruit of the Spirit."

1:12 In the past, missionaries—those who spread the Good News—boarded ships to go to foreign lands and did not expect to see their homeland shores again. Their good-byes were final, in terms of earth time. There was no turning back. While air travel, e-mail, and other technologies have made worldwide separation much easier, pioneering with the Good News still requires a high sacrifice. Paul's passion was for others to discover the Good News of eternal life through Jesus Christ, no matter what the cost would be. Pressing through frontiers of spiritual darkness still requires pioneers today—people who will reach neglected people or new people groups. Pray for missionaries, support them, join them.

● **1:12-14** Being imprisoned would cause many people to become bitter or to give up, but Paul saw it as one more opportunity to spread the Good News of Christ. Paul realized that his current circumstances weren't as important as what he did with them. Turning a bad situation into a good one, he reached out to the Roman soldiers who made up the palace guard and encouraged those Christians who were afraid of persecution. We may not be in prison, but we still have plenty of opportunities to be discouraged—times of indecision, financial burdens, family conflict,

church conflict, or the loss of our jobs. How we act in such situations will reflect what we believe. Like Paul, look for ways to demonstrate your faith even in bad situations. Whether or not the situation improves, your faith will grow stronger.

● **1:13** How did Paul end up in chains in a Roman prison? While he was visiting Jerusalem, some Jews had him arrested for preaching the Good News, but he appealed to Caesar to hear his case (Acts 21:15–25:12). He was then escorted by soldiers to Rome, where he was placed under house arrest while awaiting trial—not a trial for breaking civil law, but for proclaiming the Good News of Christ. At that time, the Roman authorities did not consider this to be a serious charge. A few years later, however, Rome would take a different view of Christianity and make every effort to stamp it out of existence. Paul's house arrest allowed him some degree of freedom. He could have visitors, continue to preach, and write letters such as this one. A brief record of Paul's time in Rome is found in Acts 28:11-31. The "palace guard" refers to the elite troops housed in the emperor's palace.

1:14 When we speak fearlessly for Christ or live faithfully for him during difficult situations, we encourage others to do the same. Be an encouragement by the way that you live.

● **1:15-18** Paul had an amazingly selfless attitude. He knew that some were preaching to build their own reputations, taking advantage of his imprisonment to try to make a name for themselves. Regardless of the motives of these preachers, Paul rejoiced that the Good News was being preached. Some Christians serve for the wrong reasons. Paul wouldn't condone, nor does God excuse, their motives, but we should be glad if God uses their message, regardless of their motives.

1:16 Paul could have become depressed, discouraged, or disillusioned. He could have wallowed in self-pity and despair. Instead, he regarded his imprisonment as being appointed by God. In fact, God had used Paul's imprisonment in Rome to bring the gospel to the center of the empire, as well as to give Paul lots of time to write letters that would one day end up in the New Testament and give us much teaching and encouragement. Do you have difficulty accepting your station in life? Do you resent where God has placed you? Although education and focused effort may enable us to take a new role or get a new job, often God puts us in a place to serve. Whether it is an actual prison or a place that feels like one, God wants you to serve him faithfully and joyfully.

genuine, the message about Christ is being preached either way, so I rejoice. And I will continue to rejoice. ¹⁹For I know that as you pray for me and the Spirit of Jesus Christ helps me, this will lead to my deliverance.

1:19
2 Cor 1:11

Paul's Life for Christ

²⁰For I fully expect and hope that I will never be ashamed, but that I will continue to be bold for Christ, as I have been in the past. And I trust that my life will bring honor to Christ, whether I live or die. ²¹For to me, living means living for Christ, and dying is even better. ²²But if I live, I can do more fruitful work for Christ. So I really don't know which is better. ²³I'm torn between two desires: I long to go and be with Christ, which would be far better for me. ²⁴But for your sakes, it is better that I continue to live.

²⁵Knowing this, I am convinced that I will remain alive so I can continue to help all of you grow and experience the joy of your faith. ²⁶And when I come to you again, you will have even more reason to take pride in Christ Jesus because of what he is doing through me.

1:20
Rom 5:5; 14:8
1 Cor 6:20
Eph 6:19
1:21
Gal 2:20
Col 1:27
1:22
Rom 1:13
1:23
2 Cor 5:8
2 Tim 4:6
1:26
Phil 2:24

Live as Citizens of Heaven

²⁷Above all, you must live as citizens of heaven, conducting yourselves in a manner worthy of the Good News about Christ. Then, whether I come and see you again or only hear about you, I will know that you are standing together with one spirit and one purpose, fighting together for the faith, which is the Good News. ²⁸Don't be intimidated in any way by your enemies. This will be a sign to them that they are going to be destroyed, but that you are going to be saved, even by God himself. ²⁹For you have been given not only the privilege of trusting in Christ but also the privilege of suffering for him. ³⁰We are in this struggle together. You have seen my struggle in the past, and you know that I am still in the midst of it.

1:27
Eph 4:1
Phil 4:1-2
1:28
2 Tim 2:11
Heb 13:6
1:29
Matt 5:11-12
1:30
Acts 16:19-40
1 Thes 2:2

2. Joy in serving

Have the Attitude of Christ

2 Is there any encouragement from belonging to Christ? Any comfort from his love? Any fellowship together in the Spirit? Are your hearts tender and compassionate? ²Then make me truly happy by agreeing wholeheartedly with each other, loving one another, and working together with one mind and purpose.

2:1
2 Cor 13:13
Col 3:12
2:2
1 Pet 3:8

• **1:19-21** This was not Paul's final imprisonment in Rome. But he didn't know that. Awaiting trial, he knew he could either be released or executed. However, he trusted Christ to work it out for his deliverance. Paul's prayer was that when he stood trial, he would speak courageously for Christ and not be timid or ashamed. Whether he lived or died, he wanted to exalt Christ. As it turned out, he was released from this imprisonment but arrested again two or three years later. Only faith in Christ could sustain Paul in such adversity.

• **1:20, 21** To those who don't believe in God, life on earth is all there is, and so it is natural for them to strive for this world's values: money, popularity, power, pleasure, and prestige. For Paul, however, to live meant to develop eternal values and to tell others about Christ, who alone could help them see life from an eternal perspective. Paul's whole purpose in life was to speak out boldly for Christ and to become more like him. Thus, Paul could confidently say that dying would be even better than living, because in death he would be removed from worldly troubles, and he would see Christ face to face (1 John 3:2, 3). If you're not ready to die, then you're not ready to live. Make certain of your eternal destiny; then you will be free to serve—devoting your life to what really counts, without fear of death.

1:24 Paul had a purpose for living when he served the Philippians and others. We also need a purpose for living that goes beyond providing for our own physical needs. Whom can you serve or help? What is your purpose for living?

1:27 Paul encouraged the believers to be unified, as they stood "side by side, fighting together for the faith, which is the Good News." How sad that much time and effort are lost in some churches by fighting against one another instead of uniting against the real opposition! It takes a courageous church to resist infighting and to maintain the common purpose of serving Christ.

• **1:29** Paul considered it a privilege to suffer for Christ. We do not by nature consider suffering a privilege. Yet when we suffer, if we faithfully represent Christ, our message and example affect us and others for good (see Acts 5:41). Suffering has these additional benefits: (1) It takes our eyes off of earthly comforts; (2) it weeds out superficial believers; (3) it strengthens the faith of those who endure; (4) it serves as an example to others who may follow us. When we suffer for our faith, it doesn't mean that we have done something wrong. In fact, the opposite is often true—it verifies that we have been faithful. Use suffering to build your character. Don't resent it or let it tear you down.

• **1:30** Throughout his life, Paul suffered for spreading the Good News. Like the Philippians, we are in conflict with anyone who would discredit the saving message of Christ. All true believers are in this fight together, uniting against the same enemy for a common cause.

Paul never urges Christians to seek suffering, as if there were virtue in pain. But we should not forget those who suffer. If your cupboard is full, share your food. If you control the wheels of power, work for justice and mercy. If you are wealthy, give generously to the poor. When life is comfortable, willingly take a share of someone else's pain, and so tell the world that the gospel is true.

• **2:1-5** Many people—even Christians—live only to make a good impression on others or to please themselves. But selfishness brings discord. Paul therefore stressed spiritual unity, asking the Philippians to love one another and to be one in spirit and purpose. When we work together, caring for the problems of others as if they were our problems, we demonstrate Christ's example of putting others first, and we experience unity. Don't be so concerned about making a good impression or meeting your own needs that you strain relationships in God's family.

2:3
Rom 12:10
Gal 5:26
1 Pet 5:5

2:4
1 Cor 10:24

2:6
John 1:1-2; 5:18

2:7
John 1:14
Rom 8:3

2:9
Eph 1:20-21
Heb 1:3-4

2:10
Isa 45:23
Rom 14:11

2:11
John 13:13

³Don't be selfish; don't try to impress others. Be humble, thinking of others as better than yourselves. ⁴Don't look out only for your own interests, but take an interest in others, too.
⁵You must have the same attitude that Christ Jesus had.

6 Though he was God,*
    he did not think of equality with God
    as something to cling to.
7 Instead, he gave up his divine privileges*;
    he took the humble position of a slave*
    and was born as a human being.
When he appeared in human form,*
8   he humbled himself in obedience to God
    and died a criminal's death on a cross.

9 Therefore, God elevated him to the place of highest honor
    and gave him the name above all other names,
10 that at the name of Jesus every knee should bow,
    in heaven and on earth and under the earth,
11 and every tongue confess that Jesus Christ is Lord,
    to the glory of God the Father.

2:6 Or *Being in the form of God.*   **2:7a** Greek *he emptied himself.*   **2:7b** Or *the form of a slave.*   **2:7c** Some English translations put this phrase in verse 8.

● **2:3** Selfishness can ruin a church, but genuine humility can build it. Being humble involves having a true perspective about ourselves (see Romans 12:3). It does not mean that we should put ourselves down. Before God, we are sinners, saved only by God's grace, but we *are* saved and therefore have great worth in God's Kingdom. We are to lay aside selfishness and treat others with respect and common courtesy. Considering others' interests as more important than our own links us with Christ, who was a true example of humility.

● **2:4** Philippi was a cosmopolitan city. The composition of the church reflected great diversity, with people from a variety of backgrounds and walks of life. Acts 16 gives us some indication of the diverse makeup of this church. The church included Lydia, a Jewish convert from Asia and a wealthy businesswoman (Acts 16:14); the slave girl (Acts 16:16, 17), probably a native Greek; and the jailer serving this colony of the empire, probably a Roman (Acts 16:25-36). With so many different backgrounds among the members, unity must have been difficult to maintain. Although there is no evidence of division in the church, its unity had to be safeguarded (3:2; 4:2). Paul encourages us to guard against any selfishness, prejudice, or jealousy that might lead to dissension. Showing genuine interest in others is a positive step forward in maintaining unity among believers.

2:5 Jesus Christ was humble, willing to give up his rights in order to obey God and serve people. Like Christ, we should have a servant's attitude, serving out of love for God and for others, not out of guilt or fear. Remember, you can choose your attitude. You can approach life expecting to be served, or you can look for opportunities to serve others. See Mark 10:45 for more on Christ's attitude of servanthood.

2:5-7 The Incarnation was the act of the preexistent Son of God voluntarily assuming a human body and human nature. Without ceasing to be God, he became a human being, the man called Jesus. He did not give up his deity to become human, but he set aside the right to his glory and power. In submission to the Father's will, Christ limited his power and knowledge. Jesus of Nazareth was subject to place, time, and many other human limitations. What made his humanity unique was his freedom from sin. In his full humanity, Jesus showed us everything about God's character that can be conveyed in human terms. The Incarnation is explained further in these passages: John 1:1-14; Romans 1:2-5; 2 Corinthians 8:9; 1 Timothy 3:16; Hebrews 2:14; and 1 John 1:1-3.

● **2:5-11** These verses are probably from a hymn sung by the early Christian church. The passage holds many parallels to the prophecy of the suffering servant in Isaiah 53. As a hymn, it was not meant to be a complete statement about the nature and work of Christ. Several key characteristics of Jesus Christ, however, are praised in this passage: (1) Christ has always existed with God; (2) Christ is equal to God because he *is* God (John 1:1ff; Colossians 1:15-19); (3) though Christ is God, he became a man in order to fulfill God's plan of salvation for all people; (4) Christ did not just have the appearance of being a man—he actually became human to identify with our sins; (5) Christ voluntarily laid aside his divine rights and privileges out of love for his Father; (6) Christ died on the cross for our sins so we wouldn't have to face eternal death; (7) God glorified Christ because of his obedience; (8) God raised Christ to his original position at the Father's right hand, where he will reign forever as our Lord and Judge. How can we do anything less than praise Christ as our Lord and dedicate ourselves to his service!

● **2:5-11** Often people excuse selfishness, pride, or evil by claiming their rights. They think, "I can cheat on this test; after all, I deserve to pass this class," or "I can spend all this money on myself—I worked hard for it," or "I can get an abortion; I have a right to control my own body." But as believers, we should have a different attitude, one that enables us to lay aside our rights in order to serve others. If we say we follow Christ, we must also say we want to live as he lived. We should develop his attitude of humility as we serve, even when we are not likely to get recognition for our efforts. Are you selfishly clinging to your rights, or are you willing to serve?

2:8 Death on a cross (crucifixion) was the form of capital punishment that Romans used for notorious criminals. It was excruciatingly painful and humiliating. Prisoners were nailed or tied to a cross and left to die. Death might not come for several days, and it usually came by suffocation when the weight of the weakened body made breathing more and more difficult. Jesus died as one who was cursed (Galatians 3:13). How amazing that the perfect man should die this most shameful death so that we would not have to face eternal punishment!

2:9-11 At the Last Judgment, even those who are condemned will recognize Jesus' authority and right to rule. People can choose now to commit their lives to Jesus as Lord or be forced to acknowledge him as Lord when he returns. Christ may return at any moment. Are you prepared to meet him?

Shine Brightly for Christ

12Dear friends, you always followed my instructions when I was with you. And now that I am away, it is even more important. Work hard to show the results of your salvation, obeying God with deep reverence and fear. 13For God is working in you, giving you the desire and the power to do what pleases him.

14Do everything without complaining and arguing, 15so that no one can criticize you. Live clean, innocent lives as children of God, shining like bright lights in a world full of crooked and perverse people. 16Hold firmly to the word of life; then, on the day of Christ's return, I will be proud that I did not run the race in vain and that my work was not useless. 17But I will rejoice even if I lose my life, pouring it out like a liquid offering to God,* just like your faithful service is an offering to God. And I want all of you to share that joy. 18Yes, you should rejoice, and I will share your joy.

2:13
Rom 8:28
1 Cor 12:6
Heb 13:21
2:14
1 Cor 10:10
2:15
Matt 5:45
John 12:36
Eph 5:1
2:16
1 Thes 2:19
2:17
Rom 15:16
2 Tim 4:6

Paul Commends Timothy

19If the Lord Jesus is willing, I hope to send Timothy to you soon for a visit. Then he can cheer me up by telling me how you are getting along. 20I have no one else like Timothy, who genuinely cares about your welfare. 21All the others care only for themselves and not for what matters to Jesus Christ. 22But you know how Timothy has proved himself. Like a son with his father, he has served with me in preaching the Good News. 23I hope to send him to you just as soon as I find out what is going to happen to me here. 24And I have confidence from the Lord that I myself will come to see you soon.

2:20
1 Cor 16:10
2:21
1 Cor 10:24
2:22
1 Cor 4:17
1 Tim 1:2
2:24
Phil 1:25

Paul Commends Epaphroditus

25Meanwhile, I thought I should send Epaphroditus back to you. He is a true brother, co-worker, and fellow soldier. And he was your messenger to help me in my need. 26I am sending him because he has been longing to see you, and he was very distressed that you heard

2:25
Phil 4:18
2:26
Phil 1:8

2:17 Greek *I will rejoice even if I am to be poured out as a liquid offering.*

• **2:12** "Work hard to show the results of your salvation," in light of the preceding exhortation to unity, may mean that the entire church was to work together to rid themselves of divisions and discord. The Philippian Christians needed to be especially careful to obey Christ, now that Paul wasn't there to continually remind them about what was right. We, too, must be careful about what we believe and how we live, especially when we are on our own. In the absence of cherished Christian leaders, we must focus our attention and devotion even more on Christ so that we won't be sidetracked.

• **2:13** What do we do when we don't feel like obeying? God has not left us alone in our struggles to do his will. He wants to come alongside us and be within us to help. God gives us the *desire* and the *power* to do what pleases him. The secret to a changed life is to submit to God's control and let him work. Next time ask God to help you *desire* to do his will.

• **2:13** To be like Christ, we must train ourselves to think like Christ. To change our desires to be more like Christ's, we need the power of the indwelling Spirit (1:19), the influence of faithful Christians, obedience to God's Word (not just exposure to it), and sacrificial service. Often it is in *doing* God's will that we gain the *desire* to do it (see 4:8, 9). Do what he wants and trust him to change your desires.

• **2:14-16** Why are complaining and arguing so harmful? If all that people know about a church is that its members constantly argue, complain, and gossip, they get a false impression of Christ and the Good News. Belief in Christ should unite those who trust him. If your church is always complaining and arguing, it lacks the unifying power of Jesus Christ. Stop arguing with other Christians or complaining about people and conditions within the church; instead, let the world see Christ.

• **2:14-16** Our lives should be characterized by moral purity, patience, and peacefulness, so that we will "shine brightly" in a dark and depraved world. A transformed life is an effective witness to the power of God's Word. Are you shining brightly, or are you clouded by complaining and arguing? Don't let dissensions snuff out your light. Shine out for God. Your role is to shine until Jesus returns and bathes the world in his radiant glory.

2:17 The drink offering was an important part of the sacrificial system of the Jews (for an explanation, see Numbers 28:7). Because this church had little Jewish background, the liquid offering may refer to the wine poured out to pagan deities prior to important public events. Paul regarded his life as a sacrifice.

• **2:17** Even if he had to die, Paul was content, knowing that he had helped the Philippians live for Christ. When you're totally committed to serving Christ, sacrificing to build the faith of others brings a joyous reward.

• **2:19, 22** When Paul wrote these words, most vocational training was done by fathers, and sons stayed loyal to the family business. Timothy displayed that same loyalty in his spiritual apprenticeship with Paul. Timothy was with Paul in Rome when Paul wrote this letter. He traveled with Paul on his second missionary journey when the church at Philippi was begun. (For more information on Timothy, see his Profile in 1 Timothy 2, p. 2059.)

Just as a skilled workman trains an apprentice, Paul was preparing Timothy to carry on the ministry in his absence. Paul encouraged younger Christians to learn, to observe, to help, and then to lead. Paul expected older Christians to teach, to model, to mentor, and then to turn over leadership. The benefits of such a process are new enthusiasm and vision, new methods and energy. Are you a teacher? Whom are you apprenticing for God's work? Are you a learner? How are you showing your eagerness to fulfill the call God has on your life?

2:21 Paul observed that most believers are too preoccupied with their own needs to spend time working for Christ. Don't let your schedule and concerns crowd out your love and Christian service to others.

• **2:23** Paul was in prison (either awaiting his trial or its verdict) for preaching about Christ. He was telling the Philippians that when he learned of the court's decision, he would send Timothy to them with the news. Paul wanted them to know that he was ready to accept whatever came (1:21-26).

• **2:25** Epaphroditus delivered money from the Philippians to Paul; then he returned with this thank-you letter to Philippi. Epaphroditus may have been an elder in Philippi (2:25-30; 4:18) who,

he was ill. 27And he certainly was ill; in fact, he almost died. But God had mercy on him—and also on me, so that I would not have one sorrow after another.

28So I am all the more anxious to send him back to you, for I know you will be glad to see him, and then I will not be so worried about you. 29Welcome him with Christian love* and with great joy, and give him the honor that people like him deserve. 30For he risked his life for the work of Christ, and he was at the point of death while doing for me what you couldn't do from far away.

3. Joy in believing
The Priceless Value of Knowing Christ

3 Whatever happens, my dear brothers and sisters,* rejoice in the Lord. I never get tired of telling you these things, and I do it to safeguard your faith.

2 Watch out for those dogs, those people who do evil, those mutilators who say you must be circumcised to be saved. 3For we who worship by the Spirit of God* are the ones who are truly circumcised. We rely on what Christ Jesus has done for us. We put no confidence in human effort, 4though I could have confidence in my own effort if anyone could. Indeed, if others have reason for confidence in their own efforts, I have even more!

5I was circumcised when I was eight days old. I am a pure-blooded citizen of Israel and a member of the tribe of Benjamin—a real Hebrew if there ever was one! I was a member of the Pharisees, who demand the strictest obedience to the Jewish law. 6I was so zealous that I harshly persecuted the church. And as for righteousness, I obeyed the law without fault.

7I once thought these things were valuable, but now I consider them worthless because

2:29 1 Cor 16:16, 18 1 Tim 5:17
2:30 1 Cor 16:17
3:1 Phil 2:18; 4:4
3:2 Ps 22:16, 20 Rev 22:15
3:3 John 4:21-24 Rom 2:29 Gal 6:15 Col 2:11
3:5 Luke 1:59; 2:21 Acts 23:6 Rom 11:1 2 Cor 11:22
3:6 Acts 8:3; 22:4; 26:9-11 Gal 1:13

2:29 Greek *in the Lord*.   **3:1** Greek *brothers;* also in 3:13, 17.   **3:3** Some manuscripts read *worship God in spirit;* one early manuscript reads *worship in spirit.*

while staying with Paul, became ill (2:27, 30). After Epaphroditus recovered, he returned home. He is mentioned only in Philippians.

2:29, 30 The world honors those who are intelligent, beautiful, rich, and powerful. What kind of people should the church honor? Paul indicates that we should honor those who give their lives for the sake of Christ, going where we cannot go ourselves. Our missionaries do that for us today by providing ministry where we are not able to go.

3:1 As a safeguard, Paul reviewed the basics with these believers. The Bible is our safeguard both morally and theologically. When we read it individually and publicly in church, it alerts us to corrections we need to make in our thoughts, attitudes, and actions.

- **3:2, 3** These "dogs" and "mutilators" were very likely Judaizers—Jewish Christians who wrongly believed that it was essential for Gentiles to follow all the Old Testament Jewish laws, especially submission to the rite of circumcision, in order to receive salvation. Many Judaizers were motivated by spiritual pride. Because they had invested so much time and effort in keeping their laws, they couldn't accept the fact that all their efforts couldn't bring them a step closer to salvation.

  Paul criticized the Judaizers because they looked at Christianity backward—thinking that what they *did* (circumcision—cutting or mutilating the flesh) made them believers rather than the free gift of grace given by Christ. What believers do is a *result* of faith, not a *prerequisite* to faith. This had been confirmed by the early church leaders at the Jerusalem council 11 years earlier (Acts 15). Who are the Judaizers of our day? They are those who say that people must add something else to simple faith. No person should add anything to Christ's offer of salvation by grace through faith.

- **3:2, 3** It is easy to place more emphasis on human effort than on internal faith, but God values the attitude of our heart above all else. Don't judge people's spirituality by their fulfillment of duties or by their level of human activity. And don't think that you will satisfy God by feverishly doing his work. God notices all you do for him and will reward you for it, but only if it comes as a loving response to his free gift of salvation.

- **3:4-6** At first glance, it looks like Paul is boasting about his achievements. But he is actually doing the opposite, showing that human achievements, no matter how impressive, cannot earn a person salvation and eternal life with God. Paul had impressive credentials: upbringing, nationality, family background, inheritance, orthodoxy, activity, and morality (see 2 Corinthians 11; Galatians 1:13-24, for more of his credentials). However, his conversion to faith in Christ (Acts 9) wasn't based on what he had done but on God's grace. Paul did not depend on his deeds to please God, because even the most impressive credentials fall short of God's holy standards. Are you depending on Christian parents, church affiliation, or just being good to make you right with God? Credentials, accomplishments, or reputation cannot earn salvation. Salvation comes only through faith in Christ.

3:5 Paul belonged to the tribe of Benjamin, a heritage greatly esteemed among the Jews. From this tribe had come Israel's first king, Saul (1 Samuel 10:20-24). The tribes of Benjamin and Judah were the only two tribes to return to Israel after the Exile (Ezra 4:1). Paul was also a Pharisee, a member of a very devout Jewish sect that scrupulously kept its own numerous rules in addition to the laws of Moses. Paul explains for these mostly Gentile believers that his Jewish credentials were impeccable.

3:6 Why had Paul, a devout Jewish leader, persecuted the church? Agreeing with the leaders of the religious establishment, Paul had thought that Christianity was heretical and blasphemous. Because Jesus did not meet his expectations of what the Messiah would be like, Paul had assumed that Jesus' claims were false—and therefore wicked. In addition, he had seen Christianity as a political menace because it threatened to disrupt the fragile harmony between the Jews and the Roman government.

3:7 When Paul spoke of "these things," he was referring to his credentials, credits, and successes. After showing that he could beat the Judaizers at their own game (being proud of who they were and what they had done), Paul showed that it was the wrong game. Be careful of considering past achievements so important that they get in the way of your relationship with Christ.

of what Christ has done. ⁸Yes, everything else is worthless when compared with the infinite value of knowing Christ Jesus my Lord. For his sake I have discarded everything else, counting it all as garbage, so that I could gain Christ ⁹and become one with him. I no longer count on my own righteousness through obeying the law; rather, I become righteous through faith in Christ.* For God's way of making us right with himself depends on faith. ¹⁰I want to know Christ and experience the mighty power that raised him from the dead. I want to suffer with him, sharing in his death, ¹¹so that one way or another I will experience the resurrection from the dead!

Pressing toward the Goal

¹²I don't mean to say that I have already achieved these things or that I have already reached perfection. But I press on to possess that perfection for which Christ Jesus first possessed me. ¹³No, dear brothers and sisters, I have not achieved it,* but I focus on this one thing: Forgetting the past and looking forward to what lies ahead, ¹⁴I press on to reach the end of the race and receive the heavenly prize for which God, through Christ Jesus, is calling us.

¹⁵Let all who are spiritually mature agree on these things. If you disagree on some point, I believe God will make it plain to you. ¹⁶But we must hold on to the progress we have already made.

3:9 Or *through the faithfulness of Christ.* 3:13 Some manuscripts read *not yet achieved it.*

3:8
John 17:3
Eph 4:13
2 Pet 3:18

3:9
Rom 1:17; 3:21-22;
9:30; 10:3
Gal 2:16

3:10
Rom 6:3-5; 8:17, 29
Gal 6:17

3:11
Acts 26:8
1 Cor 15:23
Rev 20:5-6

3:12
1 Tim 6:12, 19

3:13
Luke 9:62

3:14
1 Cor 9:24
2 Tim 4:7-8
Heb 12:1

3:15
1 Cor 2:6
Phil 1:9-10

• **3:8** After Paul considered everything he had accomplished in his life, he decided to write it all off as "worthless" when compared with the greatness of knowing Christ. We should value our relationship with Christ as more important than anything else. To know Christ should be our ultimate goal. Yet how do we know him better? (1) Study the life of Christ in the Gospels. See how Christ lived and responded to people (Matthew 11:29). (2) Study all the New Testament references to Christ (Colossians 1:15–2:15). (3) As you worship and pray, let the Holy Spirit remind you of Christ's words (John 14:26). (4) Take up Christ's mission to preach the gospel and learn from his sufferings (Matthew 28:19; Philippians 3:10).

To do these things, however, may mean that you must make major changes in your thinking and in your lifestyle. Are you willing to change your values in order to know Christ better? Will you fix or rearrange your crowded schedule in order to set aside a few minutes each day for prayer and Bible study? Will you change some of your plans, goals, and desires in order to conform with what you learn about Christ? Whatever you must change or give up, having Christ and becoming one with him will be more than worth the sacrifice.

3:9 No amount of law keeping, self-improvement, discipline, or religious effort can make us right with God. Righteousness comes only from God, and we are made righteous (receive right standing with him) by trusting in Christ. He exchanges our sin and shortcomings for his complete righteousness. See 2 Corinthians 5:21 for more on Christ's gift of righteousness.

3:9, 10 Paul gave up everything—family, friendship, and freedom—in order to know Christ and his resurrection power. We, too, have access to this knowledge and this power, but we may have to make sacrifices to enjoy it fully. What are you willing to give up in order to know Christ? A crowded schedule in order to set aside a few minutes each day for prayer and Bible study? Your friend's approval? Some of your plans or pleasures? Whatever it is, knowing Christ is more than worth the sacrifice.

• **3:10** When we become one with Christ by trusting in him, we experience the power that raised him from the dead. That same mighty power will help us live morally renewed and regenerated lives. But before we can walk in newness of life, we must die to sin. Just as the Resurrection gives us Christ's power to live for him, his crucifixion marks the death of our old sinful nature. We can't know the victory of the Resurrection without personally applying the Crucifixion.

3:11 When Paul wrote, "so that one way or another I will experience the resurrection from the dead," he was not implying uncertainty or doubt. He was unsure of the way that he would meet God, whether by execution or by natural death. He did not doubt that he would be raised, but attainment of it was within God's power and not his own.

3:11 Just as Christ was exalted after his resurrection, so we will one day share Christ's glory (Revelation 22:1-7). Paul knew that he might die soon, but he had faith that he would be raised to life again.

• **3:12-14** Paul said that his goal was to know Christ, to be like Christ, and to be all Christ had in mind for him. This goal took all of Paul's energies. This is a helpful example for us. We should not let anything take our eyes off our goal—knowing Christ. With the single-mindedness of an athlete in training, we must lay aside everything harmful and forsake anything that may distract us from being effective Christians. What is holding you back?

• **3:13, 14** Paul had reason to forget the past—he had held the coats of those who had stoned Stephen, the first Christian martyr (Acts 7:57, 58, Paul is called Saul here). We have all done things for which we are ashamed, and we live in the tension of what we have been and what we want to be. Because our hope is in Christ, however, we can let go of past guilt and look forward to what God will help us become. Don't dwell on your past. Instead, grow in the knowledge of God by concentrating on your relationship with him *now*. Realize that you are forgiven, and then move on to a life of faith and obedience. Look forward to a fuller and more meaningful life because of your hope in Christ.

3:15, 16 Sometimes trying to live a perfect Christian life can be so difficult that it leaves us drained and discouraged. We may feel so far from perfect that we think we can never please God with our life. Paul used *perfection* (3:12) to mean mature or complete, not flawless in every detail. Those who are mature should press on in the Holy Spirit's power, knowing that Christ will reveal and fill in any discrepancy between what we are and what we should be. Christ's provision is no excuse for lagging devotion, but it provides relief and assurance for those who feel driven.

3:16 Christian maturity involves acting on the guidance that you have already received. We can always make excuses that we still have so much to learn. The instruction for us is to live up to what we already know and live out what we have already learned. We do not have to be sidetracked by an unending search for truth.

3:17
1 Cor 4:16
1 Pet 5:3

3:18
Gal 6:12

3:20
Eph 2:19
Heb 12:22-23

3:21
Rom 8:29
1 Cor 15:28, 43-53

¹⁷Dear brothers and sisters, pattern your lives after mine, and learn from those who follow our example. ¹⁸For I have told you often before, and I say it again with tears in my eyes, that there are many whose conduct shows they are really enemies of the cross of Christ. ¹⁹They are headed for destruction. Their god is their appetite, they brag about shameful things, and they think only about this life here on earth. ²⁰But we are citizens of heaven, where the Lord Jesus Christ lives. And we are eagerly waiting for him to return as our Savior. ²¹He will take our weak mortal bodies and change them into glorious bodies like his own, using the same power with which he will bring everything under his control.

4:1
Phil 1:8

4 Therefore, my dear brothers and sisters,* stay true to the Lord. I love you and long to see you, dear friends, for you are my joy and the crown I receive for my work.

4:1 Greek *brothers;* also in 4:8.

THREE STAGES OF PERFECTION

1. Perfect Relationship   We are perfect because of our eternal union with the infinitely perfect Christ. When we become his children, we are declared "not guilty" and thus righteous because of what Christ, God's beloved Son, has done for us. This perfection is absolute and unchangeable, and it is this perfect relationship that guarantees that we will one day be "completely perfect" (below). See Colossians 2:8-10; Hebrews 10:8-14.

2. Perfect Progress   We can grow and mature spiritually as we continue to trust Christ, learn more about him, draw closer to him, and obey him. Our progress is changeable (in contrast to our relationship, above) because it depends on our daily walk—at times in life we mature more than at other times. But we are growing toward perfection if we "press on" (Philippians 3:12). These good deeds do not perfect us; rather, as God perfects us, we do good deeds for him. See Philippians 3:1-15.

3. Completely Perfect   When Christ returns to take us into his eternal Kingdom, we will be glorified and made completely perfect. See Philippians 3:20, 21.

All phases of perfection are grounded in faith in Christ and what he has done, not what we can do for him. We cannot perfect ourselves; only God can work in and through us to "continue his work until it is finally finished on the day when Christ Jesus returns" (1:6).

• **3:17** Paul challenged the Philippians to pursue Christlikeness by following Paul's own pattern or example. This did not mean, of course, that they should copy everything he did; he had just stated that he was not perfect (3:12). But as he focused his life on being like Christ, so should they. The Gospels may not yet have been in circulation, so Paul could not tell them to read the Bible to see what Christ was like. Therefore, he urged them to imitate him. That Paul could tell people to follow his example is a testimony to his character. Can you do the same? What kind of follower would a new Christian become if he or she imitated you?

• **3:17-21** Paul criticized not only the Judaizers (see the first note on 3:2, 3) but also self-indulgent Christians, people who claimed to be Christians but didn't live up to Christ's model of servanthood and self-sacrifice. Such people satisfy their own desires before even thinking about the needs of others. Freedom in Christ does not mean freedom to be selfish. It means taking every opportunity to serve and to become the best person you can be.

3:19 Paul gets tough with people who live to appease their appetites, who believe so strongly in their greatness that they become slaves to pride. What horrible people these must be—so concerned with earthly trivia that during worship their minds wander; so consumed with work that worship is inconvenient; so busy planning the next party that there is no time for prayer. Paul says they are headed for destruction because all they can think about is this life here on earth.

But then we must ask ourselves: Is too much of our time spent on efforts that will not endure in eternity, seeking earthly pleasures, or satisfying our physical desires? We must set our minds on knowing Christ, not on the pursuits of this world.

• **3:20** Citizens of a Roman colony were expected to promote the interests of Rome and maintain the dignity of the city. In the same way, citizens of heaven ought to promote heaven's interests on earth and lead lives worthy of heavenly citizenship. Too many Christians have failed to transfer their citizenship to heaven. They still seek earthly pleasures and treasures instead of heavenly ones. Paul told the Colossians to remember that they are citizens of heaven, where the Lord Jesus Christ lives. Have you transferred your citizenship? How are you promoting heaven's interests?

3:21 The phrase "weak mortal bodies" does not imply any negative attitude toward the human body. However, the bodies we will receive when we are raised from the dead will be glorious, like Christ's resurrected body. Those who struggle with pain, physical limitations, or disabilities can have wonderful hope in the resurrection. For a more detailed discussion of our new bodies, see 1 Corinthians 15:35ff and 2 Corinthians 5:1-10.

4:1 How do we "stay true to the Lord"? This refers to what Paul has just taught in 3:20, 21. The way to stay true is to keep our eyes on Christ, to remember that this world is not our home, and to focus on the fact that Christ will bring everything under his control. Staying true means steadfastly resisting the negative influences of temptation, false teaching, or persecution. It requires perseverance when we are challenged or opposed. Don't lose heart or give up. God promises to give us strength of character. With the Holy Spirit's help and with the help of fellow believers, you can stay true to the Lord.

4. Joy in giving

Words of Encouragement

²Now I appeal to Euodia and Syntyche. Please, because you belong to the Lord, settle your disagreement. ³And I ask you, my true partner,* to help these two women, for they worked hard with me in telling others the Good News. They worked along with Clement and the rest of my co-workers, whose names are written in the Book of Life.

4:2
Phil 2:2

⁴Always be full of joy in the Lord. I say it again—rejoice! ⁵Let everyone see that you are considerate in all you do. Remember, the Lord is coming soon.

4:4
Phil 3:1

⁶Don't worry about anything; instead, pray about everything. Tell God what you need, and thank him for all he has done. ⁷Then you will experience God's peace, which exceeds anything we can understand. His peace will guard your hearts and minds as you live in Christ Jesus.

4:5
Heb 10:37
Jas 5:8-9

4:6
Matt 6:25
1 Pet 5:7

⁸And now, dear brothers and sisters, one final thing. Fix your thoughts on what is true, and honorable, and right, and pure, and lovely, and admirable. Think about things that are excellent and worthy of praise. ⁹Keep putting into practice all you learned and received from me—everything you heard from me and saw me doing. Then the God of peace will be with you.

4:7
Isa 26:3
John 14:27

4:9
Rom 15:33; 16:20
1 Cor 14:33
1 Thes 5:23

Paul's Thanks for Their Gifts

¹⁰How I praise the Lord that you are concerned about me again. I know you have always been concerned for me, but you didn't have the chance to help me. ¹¹Not that I was ever in

4:11
1 Tim 6:6

4:3 Or *loyal Syzygus.*

• **4:2, 3** Paul did not warn the Philippian church of doctrinal errors, but he did address some relational problems. These two women had been workers for Christ in the church. Their broken relationship was no small matter, because many had become believers through their efforts. It is possible to believe in Christ, work hard for his Kingdom, and yet have broken relationships with others who are committed to the same cause. But there is no excuse for remaining unreconciled. Do you need to be reconciled to someone today? If you're facing a conflict you can't resolve, don't let the tension build into an explosion. Don't withdraw or resort to cruel power plays. Don't stand idly by and wait for the dispute to resolve itself. Instead, seek the help of those known for peacemaking.

4:3 The identity of this "true partner" remains a mystery. It could be Epaphroditus, the bearer of this letter, or a comrade of Paul in prison. It could also be someone named Syzygus, another way to understand the word for "partner."

4:3 Those "whose names are written in the Book of Life" are all who are marked for salvation through their faith in Christ (see also Luke 10:17-20; Revelation 20:11-15).

• **4:4** It seems strange that a man in prison would be telling a church to rejoice. But Paul's attitude teaches us an important lesson: Our inner attitudes do not have to reflect our outward circumstances. Paul was full of joy because he knew that no matter what happened to him, Jesus Christ was with him. Several times in this letter Paul urged the Philippians to be joyful, probably because they needed to hear this. It's easy to get discouraged about unpleasant circumstances or to take unimportant events too seriously. If you haven't been joyful lately, you may not be looking at life from the right perspective.

4:4, 5 Ultimate joy comes from Christ dwelling within us. Christ is near, and at his second coming we will fully realize this ultimate joy. He who lives within us will fulfill his final purposes for us.

4:5 We are to be considerate (reasonable, fair minded, and charitable) to those outside the church, and not just to fellow believers. This means we are not to seek revenge against those who treat us unfairly, nor are we to be overly vocal about our personal rights.

• **4:6, 7** Imagine never worrying about anything! It seems like an impossibility; we all have worries on the job, in our homes, at school. But Paul's advice is to turn our worries into prayers.

Do you want to worry less? Then pray more! Whenever you start to worry, stop and pray.

• **4:7** God's peace is different from the world's peace (see John 14:27). True peace is not found in positive thinking, in absence of conflict, or in good feelings. It comes from knowing that God is in control. Our citizenship in Christ's Kingdom is sure, our destiny is set, and we can have victory over sin. Let God's peace guard your heart against anxiety.

• **4:8** What we put into our mind determines what comes out in our words and actions. Paul tells us to program our mind with thoughts that are true, honorable, right, pure, lovely, admirable, excellent, and worthy of praise. Do you have problems with impure thoughts and daydreams? Examine what you are putting into your mind through television, Internet, books, conversations, movies, and magazines. Replace harmful input with wholesome material. Above all, read God's Word and pray. Ask God to help you focus your mind on what is good and pure. It takes practice, but it can be done.

4:9 It's not enough to hear or read the Word of God or even to know it well. We must also put it into practice. How easy it is to listen to a sermon and forget what the preacher said. How easy it is to read the Bible and not think about how to live differently. How easy it is to debate what a passage means and not live out that meaning. Exposure to God's Word is not enough. It must lead to obedience.

• **4:10** In 1 Corinthians 9:11-18, Paul wrote that he didn't accept gifts from the Corinthian church because he didn't want to be accused of preaching only to get money. But Paul maintained that it was a church's responsibility to support God's ministers (1 Corinthians 9:14). He accepted the Philippians' gift because they gave it willingly and because he was in need.

• **4:10-14** Are you able to get along happily (be content) in any circumstances you face? Paul knew how to be satisfied whether he had plenty or whether he was in need. The secret was drawing on Christ's power for strength. Do you have great needs, or are you dissatisfied because you don't have what you want? Learn to rely on God's promises and Christ's power to help you be content. If you always want more, ask God to remove that desire and teach you how to be satisfied in every circumstance. He will supply all your needs, but in a way that he knows is best for you. (See the note on 4:19 for more on God supplying our needs.)

4:12
1 Cor 4:11
2 Cor 11:9
4:13
2 Cor 12:9-10
4:15
2 Cor 11:8-9
Phil 1:5
4:16
Acts 17:1
1 Thes 2:9
4:17
1 Cor 9:11
4:18
2 Cor 9:12
Phil 2:25

need, for I have learned how to be content with whatever I have. [12]I know how to live on almost nothing or with everything. I have learned the secret of living in every situation, whether it is with a full stomach or empty, with plenty or little. [13]For I can do everything through Christ,* who gives me strength. [14]Even so, you have done well to share with me in my present difficulty.

[15]As you know, you Philippians were the only ones who gave me financial help when I first brought you the Good News and then traveled on from Macedonia. No other church did this. [16]Even when I was in Thessalonica you sent help more than once. [17]I don't say this because I want a gift from you. Rather, I want you to receive a reward for your kindness.

[18]At the moment I have all I need—and more! I am generously supplied with the gifts you sent me with Epaphroditus. They are a sweet-smelling sacrifice that is acceptable and

4:13 Greek *through the one.*

TRAINING FOR THE CHRISTIAN LIFE	Reference	Metaphors	Training	Our Goal as Believers
As a great amount of training is needed for athletic activities, so we must train diligently for the Christian life. Such training takes time, dedication, energy, continued practice, and vision. We must all commit ourselves to the Christian life, but we must first know the rules as prescribed in God's Word (2 Timothy 2:5).	1 Corinthians 9:24-27	Race	Go into strict training in order to get the prize.	We train ourselves to run the race of life. So we keep our eyes on Christ—the goal—and don't get sidetracked or slowed down. When we do this, we will win a reward in Christ's Kingdom.
	Philippians 3:13, 14	Race	Focus all your energies toward winning the race.	Living the Christian life demands all of our energies. We can forget the past and strain to reach the goal because we know Christ promises eternity with him at the race's end.
	1 Timothy 4:7-10	Training	Training for godliness will help you grow in faith and character.	Just as we exercise to keep physically fit, we must also train ourselves to be spiritually fit. As our faith develops, we become better Christians, living in accordance with God's will. Such a life will attract others to Christ and pay dividends in both this life and the next.
	2 Timothy 4:7, 8	Fight, Race	Fighting the good fight and persevering to the end.	The Christian life is a fight against evil forces from without and temptation from within. If we stay true to God through it all, he promises an end, a rest, and a crown.

• **4:12, 13** Paul could get along happily because he could see life from God's point of view. He focused on what he was supposed to *do*, not what he felt he should *have*. Paul had his priorities straight, and he was grateful for everything God had given him. Paul had detached himself from the nonessentials so that he could concentrate on the eternal. Often the desire for more or better possessions is really a longing to fill an empty place in a person's life. To what are you drawn when you feel empty inside? How can you find true contentment? The answer lies in your perspective, your priorities, and your source of power.

4:13 Can we really do everything? The power we receive in union with Christ is sufficient to do his will and to face the challenges that arise from our commitment to doing it. He does not grant us superhuman ability to accomplish anything we can imagine without regard to his interests. As we contend for the faith, we will face troubles, pressures, and trials. As they come, ask Christ to strengthen you.

4:14 The Philippians shared in Paul's financial support while he was in prison.

4:15 What makes money so magnetic and giving it away so stressful? Money measures our energy; it represents our day-to-day security. Giving money away puts our work and our futures at risk. Not every charity deserves your attention, and you're wise to scrutinize missionary appeals as well. But

once you've determined that a project honors the Lord, don't hold back—give generously and joyfully. Like the Philippians, you'll be establishing an eternal partnership.

• **4:17** When we give to those in need, it not only benefits the receiver but it benefits us as well. It was not the Philippians' gift but their spirit of love and devotion that Paul appreciated most.

• **4:18** Paul was not referring to a sin offering but to a peace offering, "a sweet-smelling sacrifice that is acceptable and pleasing to God" (Leviticus 7:12-15 contains the instructions for such offerings of thanksgiving). Although the Greek and Roman Christians were not Jews and they had not offered sacrifices according to the Old Testament laws, they were well acquainted with the pagan rituals of offering sacrifices.

pleasing to God. [19]And this same God who takes care of me will supply all your needs from his glorious riches, which have been given to us in Christ Jesus.

[20]Now all glory to God our Father forever and ever! Amen.

Paul's Final Greetings

[21]Give my greetings to each of God's holy people—all who belong to Christ Jesus. The brothers who are with me send you their greetings. [22]And all the rest of God's people send you greetings, too, especially those in Caesar's household.

[23]May the grace of the Lord Jesus Christ be with your spirit.

4:19
Ps 23:1
2 Cor 9:8

4:20
Rom 11:36

4:22
Phil 1:13

4:23
Rom 16:20
Gal 6:18
2 Tim 4:22

• **4:19** We can trust that God will always meet our needs. Whatever we need on earth he will always supply, even if it is the courage to face death as Paul did. Whatever we need in heaven he will supply. We must remember, however, the difference between our wants and our needs. Most people want to feel good and avoid discomfort or pain. We may not get all that we want. By trusting in Christ, our attitudes and appetites can change from wanting everything to accepting his provision and power to live for him.

• **4:22** There were many Christians in Rome; some were even in Caesar's household. Perhaps Paul, while awaiting trial, was making converts of the Roman civil service! Paul sent greetings from these Roman Christians to the believers at Philippi. The Good News had spread to all strata of society, linking people who had no other bond but Christ. The Roman Christians and the Philippian Christians were brothers and sisters because of

their unity in Christ. Believers today are also linked to others across cultural, economic, and social barriers. Because all believers are brothers and sisters in Christ, let us live like God's true family.

• **4:23** In many ways the Philippian church was a model congregation. It was made up of many different kinds of people who were learning to work together. But Paul recognized that problems could arise, so in his thank-you letter he prepared the Philippians for difficulties that could crop up within a body of believers. Although a prisoner in Rome, Paul had learned the true secret of joy and peace—imitating Christ and serving others. By focusing our mind on Christ, we will learn unity, humility, joy, and peace. We will also be motivated to live for him. We can live confidently for him because we have "the grace of the Lord Jesus Christ" with us.

COLOSSIANS

COLOSSIANS

REMOVE the head coach, and the team flounders; break the fuel line, and the car won't run; unplug the electrical appliance, and it has no power. Whether for leadership, power, or life, connections are vital!

Colossians is a book of connections. Writing from prison in Rome, Paul combatted false teachings, which had infiltrated the Colossian church. The problem was "syncretism," combining ideas from other philosophies and religions (such as paganism, strains of Judaism, and Greek thought) with Christian truth. The resulting heresy later became known as "Gnosticism," emphasizing special knowledge (*gnosis* in Greek) and denying Christ as God and Savior. To combat this devious error, Paul stressed Christ's deity—his connection with the Father—and his sacrificial death on the cross for sin. Only by being connected with Christ through faith can anyone have eternal life, and only through a continuing connection with him can anyone have power for living. Christ is God incarnate and the *only* way to forgiveness and peace with God the Father. Paul also emphasized believers' connections with each other as Christ's body on earth.

Paul's introduction to the Colossians includes a greeting, a note of thanksgiving, and a prayer for spiritual wisdom and strength for these brothers and sisters in Christ (1:1–12). He then moves into a doctrinal discussion of the person and work of Christ (1:13–23), stating that Christ is "the visible image of the invisible God" (1:15), the Creator (1:16), "the head of the church, which is his body" (1:18), and "supreme over all who rise from the dead" (1:18). His death on the cross makes it possible for us to stand in the presence of God (1:22).

Paul then explains how the world's teachings are totally empty when compared with God's plan, and he challenges the Colossians to reject shallow answers and to live in union with Christ (1:24—2:23).

Against this theological backdrop, Paul turns to practical considerations—what the divinity, death, and resurrection of Jesus should mean to all believers (3:1–4:6). Because our eternal destiny is sure, heaven should fill our thoughts (3:1–4), sexual impurity and other worldly lusts should not be named among us (3:5–8), and truth, love, and peace should mark our lives (3:9–15). Our love for Christ should also translate into love for others—friends, fellow believers, spouses, children, parents, slaves, and masters (3:16—4:1). We should constantly communicate with God through prayer (4:2–4), and we should take every opportunity to tell others the Good News (4:5, 6). In Christ we have everything we need for salvation and for living the Christian life.

Paul had probably never visited Colosse, so he concludes this letter with personal comments about their common Christian associations, providing a living lesson of the connectedness of the body of Christ.

Read Colossians as a book for an embattled church in the first century, but read it also for its timeless truths. Gain a fresh appreciation for Christ as the *fullness* of God and the *only* source for living the Christian life. Know that he is your leader, head, and power source, and make sure of your connection to him.

VITAL STATISTICS

PURPOSE:
To combat errors in the church and to show that believers have everything they need in Christ

AUTHOR:
Paul

ORIGINAL AUDIENCE:
The church at Colosse, a city in Asia Minor

DATE WRITTEN:
Approximately A.D. 60, during Paul's imprisonment in Rome

SETTING:
Paul had never visited Colosse. Evidently the church had been founded by Epaphras and other converts from Paul's missionary travels. The church, however, had been infiltrated by religious relativism, with some believers attempting to combine elements of paganism and secular philosophy with Christian doctrine. Paul confronts these false teachings and affirms the sufficiency of Christ.

KEY VERSES:
"For in Christ lives all the fullness of God in a human body. So you also are complete through your union with Christ, who is the head over every ruler and authority" (2:9, 10).

KEY PEOPLE:
Paul, Timothy, Tychicus, Onesimus, Aristarchus, Mark, Epaphras

KEY PLACES:
Colosse, Laodicea (4:15, 16)

SPECIAL FEATURES:
Christ is presented as having absolute supremacy and sole sufficiency. Colossians has similarities to Ephesians, probably because it was written at about the same time, but it has a different emphasis.

THE BLUEPRINT

1. What Christ has done
   (1:1—2:23)
2. What Christians should do
   (3:1—4:18)

In this letter Paul clearly teaches that Christ has paid for sin, that Christ has reconciled us to God, and that Christ gives us the pattern and the power to grow spiritually. Because in Christ lives all the fullness of God, when we learn what he is like, we see what we need to become. Since Christ is Lord over all creation, we should crown him Lord over our lives. Since Christ is the head of the body, his church, we should nurture our vital connection to him.

MEGATHEMES

THEME	EXPLANATION	IMPORTANCE
Christ Is God	Jesus Christ is God in the flesh, Lord of all creation, and Lord of the new creation. He is the visible image of the invisible God. He is eternal, preexistent, omnipotent, equal with the Father. He is supreme and complete.	Because Christ is supreme, our lives must be Christ-centered. To recognize him as God means to regard our relationship with him as most vital and to make his interests our top priority.
Christ Is Head of the Church	Because Christ is God, he is the head of the church, his true believers. Christ is the founder, the leader, and the highest authority on earth. He requires first place in all our thoughts and activities.	To acknowledge Christ as our head, we must welcome his leadership in all we do or think. No person, group, or church can regard any loyalty as more critical than that of loyalty to Christ.
Union with Christ	Because our sin has been forgiven and we have been reconciled to God, we have a union with Christ that can never be broken. In our faith connection with him, we identify with his death, burial, and resurrection.	We should live in constant contact and communication with God. When we do, we all will be unified with Christ and with one another.
Heresy	False teachers were promoting a heresy that stressed self-made rules (legalism). They also sought spiritual growth by discipline of the body (asceticism) and visions (mysticism). This search created pride in their self-centered efforts.	We must not cling to our own ideas and try to blend them into Christianity. Nor should we let our hunger for a more fulfilling Christian experience cause us to trust in a teacher, a group, or a system of thought more than in Christ himself. Christ is our hope and our true source of wisdom.

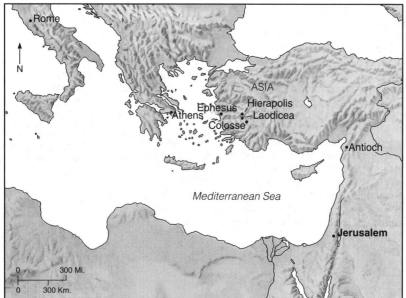

LOCATION OF COLOSSE

Paul had no doubt been through Laodicea on his third missionary journey, as it lay on the main route to Ephesus, but he had never been to Colosse. Though a large city with a significant population, Colosse was smaller and less important than the nearby cities of Laodicea and Hierapolis.

1. What Christ has done

Greetings from Paul

1:1
1 Cor 1:1
Eph 1:1

1 This letter is from Paul, chosen by the will of God to be an apostle of Christ Jesus, and from our brother Timothy.

1:2
Rom 1:7

2 We are writing to God's holy people in the city of Colosse, who are faithful brothers and sisters* in Christ.

May God our Father give you grace and peace.

Paul's Thanksgiving and Prayer

3 We always pray for you, and we give thanks to God, the Father of our Lord Jesus Christ.

1:4
Eph 1:15

4 For we have heard of your faith in Christ Jesus and your love for all of God's people,

1:2 Greek *faithful brothers.*

THE COLOSSIAN HERESY

Paul answered the various tenets of the Colossian heresy that threatened the church. This heresy was a "mixed bag," containing elements from several different heresies, some of which contradicted each other (as the chart shows).

The Heresy	Reference	Paul's Answer
Spirit is good; matter is evil.	1:15-20	God created heaven and earth for his glory.
One must follow ceremonies, rituals, and restrictions in order to be saved or perfected.	2:11, 16-23; 3:11	These were only shadows that ended when Christ came. He is all you need to be saved.
One must deny the body and live in strict asceticism.	2:18-23	Asceticism is no help in conquering evil thoughts and desires; instead, it leads to pride.
Angels must be worshiped.	2:18	Angels are not to be worshiped; Christ alone is worthy of worship.
Christ could not be both human and divine.	1:15-20; 2:2, 3	Christ is God in the flesh; he is the eternal one, head of the body, first in everything, supreme.
One must obtain "secret knowledge" in order to be saved or perfected—and this was not available to everyone.	2:2, 18	God's mysterious plan is Christ himself, and he has been revealed to all.
One must adhere to human wisdom, tradition, and philosophies.	2:4, 8-10; 3:15-17	By themselves, these can be misleading and shallow because they have human origin; instead, we should remember what Christ taught and follow his words as our ultimate authority.
It is even better to combine aspects of several religions.	2:10	You are complete through your union with Christ; he is all-sufficient.
There is nothing wrong with immorality.	3:1-11	Get rid of sin and evil because you have been chosen by God to live a new life as a representative of the Lord Jesus.

1:1 Colossians, along with Philippians, Ephesians, and Philemon, is called a "Prison Letter" because Paul wrote it from prison in Rome. This prison was actually a house where Paul was kept under close guard at all times (probably chained to a soldier) but given certain freedoms not offered to most prisoners. He was allowed to write letters and to see any visitors he wanted to see.

1:1 Paul was an apostle "chosen by the will of God." Paul often would establish his credentials as chosen and sent by God because he had not been one of the original 12 disciples. *Apostle* means "one sent out by God to preach the gospel." "Chosen by the will of God" means that he was appointed; this was not just a matter of his own personal aspirations.

• **1:1** Paul mentions Timothy in other New Testament letters as well: 2 Corinthians, Philippians, 1 and 2 Thessalonians, and Philemon. Paul also wrote two letters to Timothy (1 and 2 Timothy). For more information on these men, two of the greatest missionaries of the early church, see Paul's Profile in Acts 9, p. 1837 and Timothy's Profile in 1 Timothy 2, p. 2059.

1:2 The city of Colosse was 100 miles east of Ephesus on the Lycus River. It was not as influential as the nearby city of Laodicea, but as a trading center, it was a crossroads for ideas and religions. Colosse had a large Jewish population—many Jews had fled there

when they were forced out of Jerusalem under the persecutions of Antiochus III and IV, almost 200 years before Christ. The church in Colosse had been founded by Epaphras (1:7), one of Paul's converts. Paul had not yet visited this church. His purpose in writing was to refute heretical teachings about Christ that had been causing confusion among the Christians there.

• **1:2, 3** Letters in Paul's day frequently would begin with identifying the writer and the readers, followed by a greeting of peace. Paul usually would add Christian elements to his greetings, reminding his readers of his call by God to spread the Good News, emphasizing that the authority for his words came from God, and giving thanks for God's blessings.

• **1:4, 5** Throughout this letter Paul combats a heresy similar to Gnosticism (see the notes on 1:9-14; 1:15-23; 2:4ff). Gnostics believed that it took special knowledge to be accepted by God; for them, even for those who claimed to be Christians, Christ alone was not the way of salvation (1:20). In his introductory comments, therefore, Paul commended the Colossians for their faith, love, and hope as they looked forward to heaven (see 1 Corinthians 13:13). He deliberately omitted the word *knowledge* because of the "special knowledge" aspect of the heresy. It is not *what* we know that brings salvation but *whom* we know. Knowing Christ is knowing God.

⁵which come from your confident hope of what God has reserved for you in heaven. You have had this expectation ever since you first heard the truth of the Good News.

⁶This same Good News that came to you is going out all over the world. It is bearing fruit everywhere by changing lives, just as it changed your lives from the day you first heard and understood the truth about God's wonderful grace.

⁷You learned about the Good News from Epaphras, our beloved co-worker. He is Christ's faithful servant, and he is helping us on your behalf.* ⁸He has told us about the love for others that the Holy Spirit has given you.

⁹So we have not stopped praying for you since we first heard about you. We ask God to give you complete knowledge of his will and to give you spiritual wisdom and understanding. ¹⁰Then the way you live will always honor and please the Lord, and your lives will produce every kind of good fruit. All the while, you will grow as you learn to know God better and better.

¹¹We also pray that you will be strengthened with all his glorious power so you will have all the endurance and patience you need. May you be filled with joy,* ¹²always thanking the Father. He has enabled you to share in the inheritance that belongs to his people, who live in the light. ¹³For he has rescued us from the kingdom of darkness and transferred us into the Kingdom of his dear Son, ¹⁴who purchased our freedom* and forgave our sins.

Christ Is Supreme

¹⁵ Christ is the visible image of the invisible God.
   He existed before anything was created and is supreme over all creation,*

1:5 Eph 1:13; 1 Pet 1:4
1:6 Rom 1:13
1:7 Col 4:12; Phlm 1:23
1:9 Eph 1:15-17
1:10 Eph 4:1; Phil 1:27; 1 Thes 2:12
1:11 Eph 3:16
1:12 Acts 26:18; Eph 5:20
1:13 Matt 3:17; Acts 26:18; Eph 1:6; 2:2; 6:12
1:14 Eph 1:7
1:15 John 1:1, 18; 14:9; 2 Cor 4:4; Heb 1:3; Rev 3:14

1:7 Or *he is ministering on your behalf;* some manuscripts read *he is ministering on our behalf.* **1:11** Or *all the patience and endurance you need with joy.* **1:14** Some manuscripts add *with his blood.* **1:15** Or *He is the firstborn of all creation.*

1:5 We can have "confident hope" of what God has for us in heaven because we know that our future destination and salvation are sure (1 Peter 1:3, 4). We are free to live for Christ and love others. When you find yourself doubting or wavering in your faith or love, remember your destination—heaven.

● **1:6** Wherever Paul went, he preached the Good News—to Gentile audiences, to hostile Jewish leaders, and even to his Roman guards. Whenever people believed in the message that Paul spoke, they were changed. God's Word is not just for our information, it is for our transformation! Becoming a Christian means beginning a whole new relationship with God, not just turning over a new leaf or determining to do right. New believers have a changed purpose, direction, attitude, and behavior. They are no longer seeking to serve themselves, but they are bearing fruit for God. How is the Good News reaching others through your life?

1:7 Epaphras had founded the church at Colosse while Paul was living in Ephesus (Acts 19:10). Epaphras may have been converted in Ephesus, and then he returned to Colosse, his hometown. For some reason, he visited Rome and, while there, told Paul about the problem of the Colossian heresy. This prompted Paul to write this letter. Epaphras is also mentioned in Philemon 1:23 (the Colossian church met in Philemon's house).

● **1:8** Because of their love for one another, Christians can have an impact that goes far beyond their neighborhoods and communities. Christian love comes from the Holy Spirit (see Galatians 5:22). The Bible speaks of it as an action and attitude, not just an emotion. Love is a by-product of our new life in Christ (see Romans 5:5; 1 Corinthians 13). Christians have no excuse for not loving, because Christian love is a decision to *act* in the best interests of others.

● **1:9-14** Paul was exposing a heresy in the Colossian church that was similar to Gnosticism (see the note on 2:4ff for more information). Gnostics valued the accumulation of knowledge, but Paul pointed out that knowledge in itself is empty. To be worth anything, it must lead to a changed life and right living. His prayer for the Colossians has two dimensions: (1) that they might have complete knowledge of God's will and have spiritual wisdom and understanding; (2) that their lives would produce every kind of good fruit, even as they learned to know God better and better. Knowledge is not merely to be accumulated; it should give us

direction for living. Paul wanted the Colossians to be wise, but he also wanted them to *use* their knowledge. Knowledge of God is not a secret that only a few can discover; it is open to everyone. God wants us to learn more about him, and also to put belief into practice by helping others.

● **1:9-14** Sometimes we wonder how to pray for missionaries and other leaders we have never met. Paul had never met the Colossians, but he faithfully prayed for them. His prayers teach us how to pray for others, whether we know them or not. We can request that they (1) understand what God wants them to do, (2) gain spiritual wisdom, (3) honor and please God, (4) produce every kind of good fruit, (5) learn to know God better and better, (6) be strengthened with God's glorious power, (7) have great endurance and patience, (8) be filled with joy, and (9) give thanks always. All believers have these same basic needs. When you don't know how to pray for someone, use Paul's prayer pattern for the Colossians.

● **1:12-14** Paul lists five benefits God gives all believers through Christ: (1) He has enabled us to share in his inheritance (see also 2 Corinthians 5:21); (2) he has rescued us from Satan's kingdom of darkness and made us his children (see also 2:15); (3) he has brought us into his eternal Kingdom (see also Ephesians 1:5, 6); (4) he has purchased our freedom from sin and judgment with his blood (see also Hebrews 9:12); and (5) he has forgiven all our sins (see also Ephesians 1:7). Thank God for what you have received in Christ.

● **1:13** The Colossians feared the unseen forces of darkness, but Paul says that true believers have been transferred from darkness to light, from slavery to freedom, from guilt to forgiveness, and from the power of Satan to the power of God. We have been rescued from a rebel kingdom to serve the rightful King. Our conduct should reflect our new allegiance.

● **1:15, 16** This is one of the strongest statements about the divine nature of Christ found anywhere in the Bible. Jesus is not only equal to God (Philippians 2:6), he *is* God (John 10:30, 38; 12:45; 14:1-11); as the visible image of the invisible God, he is the exact representation of God. He not only reflects God, but he reveals God to us (John 1:18; 14:9); as supreme over all creation, he has all the priority and authority. He came from heaven, not from the dust of the earth (1 Corinthians 15:47), and he is Lord of all

1:16
John 1:3
Heb 1:2

¹⁶ for through him God created everything
    in the heavenly realms and on earth.
He made the things we can see
    and the things we can't see—
such as thrones, kingdoms, rulers, and authorities in the unseen world.
    Everything was created through him and for him.
¹⁷ He existed before anything else,
    and he holds all creation together.

1:18
Acts 4:2; 26:23
Eph 1:22-23
Rev 1:5

¹⁸ Christ is also the head of the church,
    which is his body.
He is the beginning,
    supreme over all who rise from the dead.*
So he is first in everything.
¹⁹ For God in all his fullness
    was pleased to live in Christ,
²⁰ and through him God reconciled
    everything to himself.

1:18 Or *the firstborn from the dead.*

HOW TO PRAY FOR OTHER CHRISTIANS

1. Be thankful for their faith and changed lives (1:3).

2. Ask God to help them know his will (1:9).

3. Ask God to give them spiritual wisdom and understanding (1:9).

4. Ask God to help them live to honor and please him (1:10).

5. Ask God to give them more knowledge of himself (1:10).

6. Ask God to give them strength for endurance and patience (1:11).

7. Ask God to fill them with joy and thankfulness (1:11, 12).

How many people in your life could be touched if you prayed in this way?

(Romans 9:5; 10:11-13; Revelation 1:5; 17:14). He is completely holy (Hebrews 7:26-28; 1 Peter 1:19; 2:22; 1 John 3:5), and he has authority to judge the world (Romans 2:16; 2 Corinthians 5:10; 2 Timothy 4:1). Therefore, Christ is supreme over all creation, including the spirit world. We, like the Colossian believers, must believe in the deity of Jesus Christ (that Jesus is God) or our Christian faith is hollow, misdirected, and meaningless. This is a central truth of Christianity. We must oppose those who say that Jesus was merely a prophet or a good teacher.

• **1:15-23** In the Colossian church there were several misconceptions about Christ that Paul directly refuted: (1) Believing that matter is evil, false teachers argued that God would not have come to earth as a true human being in bodily form. Paul stated that Christ is the image—the exact likeness—of God and is himself God, and yet he died on the cross as a human being. (2) They believed that God did not create the world because he would not have created evil. Paul proclaimed that Jesus Christ, who was also God in the flesh, is the Creator of both heaven and earth. (3) They said that Christ was not the unique Son of God but rather one of many intermediaries between God and people. Paul explained that Christ existed before anything else and is the firstborn of those resurrected. (4) They refused to see Christ as the source of salvation, insisting that people could find God only through special and secret knowledge. In contrast, Paul openly proclaimed the way of salvation to be through Christ alone. Paul continued to bring the argument back to Christ. When we share the Good News, we, too, must keep the focus on Christ.

1:16 Because the false teachers believed that the physical world was evil, they thought that God himself could not have created it. If Christ were God, they reasoned, he would be in charge only of the spiritual world. But Paul explained that all the thrones, kingdoms, rulers, and authorities of both the spiritual and physical worlds were created by and are under the authority of Christ himself. This includes not only the government but also the spiritual

world that the heretics were so concerned about. Christ has no equal and no rival. He is the Lord of all.

1:17 God is not only the creator of the world but he is also its sustainer. In him, everything is held together, protected, and prevented from disintegrating into chaos. Because Christ is the sustainer of all life, none of us is independent from him. We are all his servants who must daily trust him to protect us, care for us, and sustain us.

1:18 Christ is "supreme over all who rise from the dead." Jesus was raised from death, and his resurrection proves his lordship over the material world. All who trust in Christ will also defeat death and rise again to live eternally with him (1 Corinthians 15:20; 1 Thessalonians 4:14). Because of Christ's death on the cross, he has been exalted and elevated to the status that was rightfully his (see Philippians 2:5-11). Because Christ is spiritually supreme in the universe, surely we should give him first place in all our thoughts and activities. See the second note on Luke 24:6, 7 for more about the significance of Christ's resurrection.

1:19 By this statement, Paul was refuting the Greek idea that Jesus could not be human and divine at the same time. Christ was fully human; he was also fully divine. Christ has always been God and always will be God. When we have Christ, we have all of God in human form. Don't diminish any aspect of Christ—either his humanity or his divinity.

• **1:20** Christ's death provided a way for all people to come to God. It cleared away the sin that keeps us from having a right relationship with our creator. This does not mean that everyone has been saved but that the way has been cleared for anyone who will trust Christ to be saved. We can have peace with God and be reconciled to him by accepting Christ, who died in our place. Is there a distance between you and the Creator? Be reconciled to God. Come to him through Christ.

He made peace with everything in heaven and on earth
by means of Christ's blood on the cross.

²¹This includes you who were once far away from God. You were his enemies, separated from him by your evil thoughts and actions. ²²Yet now he has reconciled you to himself through the death of Christ in his physical body. As a result, he has brought you into his own presence, and you are holy and blameless as you stand before him without a single fault.

²³But you must continue to believe this truth and stand firmly in it. Don't drift away from the assurance you received when you heard the Good News. The Good News has been preached all over the world, and I, Paul, have been appointed as God's servant to proclaim it.

Paul's Work for the Church

²⁴I am glad when I suffer for you in my body, for I am participating in the sufferings of Christ that continue for his body, the church. ²⁵God has given me the responsibility of serving his church by proclaiming his entire message to you. ²⁶This message was kept secret for centuries and generations past, but now it has been revealed to God's people. ²⁷For God wanted them to know that the riches and glory of Christ are for you Gentiles, too. And this is the secret: Christ lives in you. This gives you assurance of sharing his glory.

²⁸So we tell others about Christ, warning everyone and teaching everyone with all the wisdom God has given us. We want to present them to God, perfect* in their relationship to Christ. ²⁹That's why I work and struggle so hard, depending on Christ's mighty power that works within me.

2 I want you to know how much I have agonized for you and for the church at Laodicea, and for many other believers who have never met me personally. ²I want them to be encouraged and knit together by strong ties of love. I want them to have complete confidence that they understand God's mysterious plan, which is Christ himself. ³In him lie hidden all the treasures of wisdom and knowledge.

1:28 Or *mature.*

1:21
Rom 5:10
Eph 2:3, 12
1:22
Rom 7:4
Eph 1:4; 5:27
1:23
Eph 3:17
Col 1:5-6
1:24
Phil 2:17; 3:10
2 Tim 1:8
1:26
Rom 16:25-26
Eph 3:3, 5, 9-10
1:27
Rom 8:10
Eph 3:9-11
1:28
Eph 4:13
1:29
Eph 1:19; 3:7
Phil 4:13
2:1
Col 4:12-13
2:2
Matt 11:25-27
Eph 1:18-19
Col 2:19
2:3
Isa 11:2
Rom 11:33
Eph 3:8, 19

1:21 Because we were alienated from God, we were strangers to his way of thinking and were "enemies." Sin corrupted our way of thinking about God. Wrong thinking leads to sin, which further perverts and destroys our thoughts about him. When we were out of harmony with God, our natural condition was to be totally hostile to his standards. See Romans 1:21-32 for more on the perverted thinking of unbelievers.

• **1:21, 22** *No one* is good enough to save himself or herself. If we want to live eternally with Christ, we must depend totally on God's grace. This is true whether we have been murderers or honest, hardworking citizens. We have all sinned repeatedly, and *any* sin is enough to cause us to need to come to Jesus Christ for salvation and eternal life. Apart from Christ, there is no way for our sin to be forgiven and removed.

1:22 In order to answer the accusation that Jesus was only a spirit and not a true human being, Paul explained that Jesus' physical body actually died. Jesus suffered death fully as a human so that we could be assured that he died in our place. Jesus faced death as God so we can be assured that his sacrifice was complete and that he truly removed all our sin.

• **1:22, 23** The way to be free from sin is to trust Jesus Christ to take it away. We must stand firmly in the truth of the Good News, putting our confidence in Jesus alone to forgive our sins, to make us right with God, and to empower us to live the way he desires. When a judge in a court of law declares the defendant not guilty, the person is acquitted of all the accusations or charges. Legally, it is as if he or she had never been accused. When God forgives our sins, our record is wiped clean. From his perspective, it is as though we had never sinned. God's solution is available to you. No matter what you have done or what you have been like, God's forgiveness is for you.

• **1:24** Paul's statement, "I am participating in the sufferings of Christ that continue for his body, the church," may mean that suffering is unavoidable in bringing the Good News of Christ to the world. When we suffer, Christ feels it with us. But this suffer-

ing can be endured joyfully because it changes lives and brings people into God's Kingdom (see 1 Peter 4:1, 2, 12-19). For more about how Paul could rejoice despite his suffering, see the note on Philippians 1:29.

1:26, 27 The false teachers in the Colossian church believed that spiritual perfection was a secret and hidden plan that only a few privileged people could discover. Their secret plan was meant to be exclusive. Paul said that he was proclaiming the entire message of God, not just a part of the plan. He also called God's plan a "message . . . kept secret for centuries and generations past," not in the sense that only a few would understand, but because it was hidden until Christ came. Through Christ it was made open to all. God's secret plan is "Christ lives in you"—God planned to have his Son, Jesus Christ, live in the hearts of all who believe in him—even Gentiles like the Colossians. Do you know Christ? He is not hidden if you will come to him.

• **1:28, 29** The word *perfect* means "mature or complete," not "flawless." Paul wanted to see each believer mature spiritually. Like Paul, we must work wholeheartedly like an athlete, but we should not strive in our own strength alone. We have the power of God's Spirit working in us. We can learn and grow daily, motivated by love and not by fear or pride, knowing that God gives the energy to become mature.

1:28, 29 Christ's message is for everyone; so everywhere Paul and Timothy went, they brought the Good News to all who would listen. An effective presentation of the Good News includes warning and teaching. The warning is that without Christ, people are doomed to eternal separation from God. The teaching is that salvation is available through faith in Christ. As Christ works in you, tell others about him, warning and teaching them in love. Whom do you know that needs to hear this message?

2:1 Laodicea was located a few miles northwest of Colosse. Like the church at Colosse, the Laodicean church was probably founded by one of Paul's converts while Paul was staying in Ephesus (Acts 19:10). The city was a wealthy center of trade

2:5
1 Cor 5:3-4

⁴I am telling you this so no one will deceive you with well-crafted arguments. ⁵For though I am far away from you, my heart is with you. And I rejoice that you are living as you should and that your faith in Christ is strong.

Freedom from Rules and New Life in Christ

2:6
Col 1:10

2:7
Eph 3:17

2:8
Col 2:4
1 Tim 6:20

⁶And now, just as you accepted Christ Jesus as your Lord, you must continue to follow him. ⁷Let your roots grow down into him, and let your lives be built on him. Then your faith will grow strong in the truth you were taught, and you will overflow with thankfulness.

⁸Don't let anyone capture you with empty philosophies and high-sounding nonsense that come from human thinking and from the spiritual powers* of this world, rather than

2:8 Or *the spiritual principles;* also in 2:20.

SALVATION THROUGH FAITH		Religion by Self-Effort	Salvation by Faith
	Goal	Please God by our own good deeds	Trust in Christ and then live to please God
	Means	Practice, diligent service, discipline, and obedience, in hope of reward	Confess, submit, and commit ourselves to Christ's control
	Power	Good, honest effort through self-determination	The Holy Spirit in us helps us do good work for Christ's Kingdom
	Control	Self-motivation; self-control	Christ is in us; we are in Christ
	Results	Chronic guilt, apathy, depression, failure, constant desire for approval	Joy, thankfulness, love, guidance, service, forgiveness

Salvation by faith in Christ sounds too easy for many people. They would rather think that they have done something to save themselves. Their religion becomes one of self-effort that leads either to disappointment or pride, but finally to eternal death. Christ's simple way is the only way, and it alone leads to eternal life.

---

and commerce, but later Christ would criticize the believers at Laodicea for their lukewarm commitment (Revelation 3:14-22). The fact that Paul wanted this letter to be passed on to the Laodicean church (4:16) indicates that false teaching may have spread there as well. Paul was counting on ties of love to bring the churches together to stand against this heresy and to encourage each other to remain true to God's plan of salvation in Christ. Our churches should be encouraging, unified communities, committed to carrying out Christ's work.

• **2:4ff** The problem that Paul was combating in the Colossian church was similar to Gnosticism (from the Greek word for *knowledge*). This *heresy* (a teaching contrary to biblical doctrine) undermined Christianity in several basic ways: (1) It insisted that important secret knowledge was hidden from most believers; Paul, however, said that Christ provides all the knowledge we need. (2) It taught that the body was evil; Paul countered that God himself lived in a body—that is, he was embodied in Jesus Christ. (3) It contended that Christ only seemed to be human but was not; Paul insisted that Jesus was fully human and fully God.

Gnosticism became fashionable in the second century. Even in Paul's day, these ideas sounded attractive to many, and exposure to such teachings could easily seduce a church that didn't know Christian doctrine well. Similar teachings still pose significant problems for many in the church today. We combat heresy by becoming thoroughly acquainted with God's Word through personal study and sound Bible teaching.

2:4 Christian faith provides a growth track into knowledge of the truth, but along the way, how do we guard against being deceived by lies that are masquerading as "well-crafted arguments"?

If your growth track is too narrow, you become thickheaded and insular—no one can teach you a thing. Before long, you can't teach anyone around you, for no one is listening. You are isolated. Love disappears from your life.

If your track is too wide and every idea is an exciting new possibility, you'll waste a lot of time just keeping on track and risk some dangerous detours.

The key is centering on Christ and grounding yourself in his Word. Learn daily about the Savior. Study the Bible. Develop your theological knowledge. Stay humble and curious about the amazing complexity of the world God has made. Ask lots of questions about the assumptions behind ideas new to you. Press toward wisdom. Pray for understanding. God has given us minds for learning—never quit using yours.

• **2:6, 7** Receiving Christ as Lord of your life is the beginning of life with Christ. But you must continue to follow his leadership by being rooted, built up, and strengthened in the faith. Christ wants to guide you and help you with your daily problems. You can live for Christ by (1) committing your life and submitting your will to him (Romans 12:1, 2); (2) seeking to learn from him, his life, and his teachings (Colossians 3:16); and (3) recognizing the Holy Spirit's power in you (Acts 1:8; Galatians 5:22).

• **2:7** Paul uses the illustration of our being rooted in Christ. Just as plants draw nourishment from the soil through their roots, so we draw our life-giving strength from Christ. The more we draw our strength from him, the less we will be fooled by those who falsely claim to have life's answers. If Christ is our strength, we will be free from human regulations.

• **2:8** Paul writes against any philosophy of life based only on human ideas and experiences. Paul himself was a gifted philosopher, so he is not condemning philosophy. He is condemning teaching that credits humanity, not Christ, with being the answer to life's problems. That approach becomes a false religion. There are many man-made approaches to life's problems that totally disregard God. To resist heresy you must use your mind, keep your eyes on Christ, and study God's Word.

from Christ. [9]For in Christ lives all the fullness of God in a human body.* [10]So you also are complete through your union with Christ, who is the head over every ruler and authority.

[11]When you came to Christ, you were "circumcised," but not by a physical procedure. Christ performed a spiritual circumcision—the cutting away of your sinful nature.* [12]For you were buried with Christ when you were baptized. And with him you were raised to new life because you trusted the mighty power of God, who raised Christ from the dead.

[13]You were dead because of your sins and because your sinful nature was not yet cut away. Then God made you alive with Christ, for he forgave all our sins. [14]He canceled the record of the charges against us and took it away by nailing it to the cross. [15]In this way, he disarmed* the spiritual rulers and authorities. He shamed them publicly by his victory over them on the cross.

[16]So don't let anyone condemn you for what you eat or drink, or for not celebrating certain holy days or new moon ceremonies or Sabbaths. [17]For these rules are only shadows of

2:9 John 1:14, 16
2:10 Eph 1:21-22; 3:19
2:12 Rom 6:5 Eph 1:19-20; 2:6
2:13 Eph 2:1, 5
2:14 Eph 2:15 1 Pet 2:24
2:15 John 12:31 2 Cor 2:14 Eph 4:8
2:16 1 Chr 23:31 Rom 14:3, 5

2:9 Or *in him dwells all the completeness of the Godhead bodily.* **2:11** Greek *the cutting away of the body of the flesh.* **2:15** Or *he stripped off.*

2:9 Again Paul asserts Christ's deity. "In Christ lives all the fullness of God in a human body" means that all of God was in Christ's human body. When we have Christ, we have everything we need for salvation and right living. See the note on 1:15, 16 for more on the divine nature of Christ.

• **2:10** Look around you. People are searching for something to give their lives a boost. Few people seem content within themselves. A strange and often hard-to-identify inner vacuum gives most people an uneasy sense of incompleteness. Christ fills that vacuum! As Jesus' person is fully divine, so we, united by faith to Jesus, find personal fulfillment in him: "You also are complete through your union with Christ."

When you know Jesus Christ, you don't need to seek God by means of other religions, cults, or unbiblical philosophies as the Colossians were doing. Christ alone holds the answers to the true meaning of life because he *is* life. Christ is the unique source of knowledge and power for the Christian life. No Christian needs anything in addition to what Christ has provided to be saved. Some days may not feel like it, but in Jesus, the vacuum is gone; the full power and presence of God have taken up residence in your mind and heart. You are a new person, equipped for life and satisfied in God. Take some risks—God will guide you. Give more generously—God will supply. Love more freely—God will energize you. Say "can do" more often—God will amaze you.

2:11 Jewish males were circumcised as a sign of the Jews' covenant with God (Genesis 17:9-14). With the death of Christ, circumcision was no longer necessary. So now our commitment to God is written on our heart, not our body. Christ sets us free from our evil desires by a spiritual operation, not a bodily one. God removes the old nature and gives us a new nature.

• **2:11, 12** In this passage, circumcision is related to baptism; therefore, some see baptism as the New Testament sign of the covenant, identifying the person with the covenant community. Baptism parallels the death, burial, and resurrection of Christ, and it also portrays the death and burial of our sinful old way of life followed by resurrection to new life in Christ. Remembering that our old sinful life is dead and buried with Christ gives us a powerful motive to resist sin. Not wanting the desires of our past to come back to power again, we can consciously choose to treat our desires as if they were dead. Then we can continue to enjoy our wonderful new life with Christ (see Galatians 3:27 and Colossians 3:1-4).

• **2:13-15** Before we believed in Christ, our nature was evil. We disobeyed, rebelled, and ignored God (even at our best, we did not love him with all our heart, soul, and mind). The Christian, however, has a new nature. God has crucified the old rebellious nature (Romans 6:6) and replaced it with a new loving nature (Colossians 3:9, 10). The penalty of sin died with Christ on the cross. God has declared us not guilty, and we need no longer live under sin's power. God does not take us out of the world or make us robots—we will still feel like sinning, and sometimes we will

sin. The difference is that before we were saved, we were slaves to our sinful nature; but now we are free to live for Christ (see Galatians 2:20).

2:14 The record that was canceled contained the legal demands of the Old Testament law. The law opposed us by its demands for payment for our sin. Although no one can be saved by merely keeping that record, the moral truths and principles in the Old Testament still teach and guide today.

2:14 We can enjoy our new lives in Christ because we have joined him in his death and resurrection. Our evil desires, our bondage to sin, and our love of sin died with him. Now, joining him in his resurrection life, we may have unbroken fellowship with God and freedom from sin. Our debt for sin has been paid in full; our sins are swept away and forgotten by God; and we can be clean and new. For more on the difference between our new life in Christ and our old sinful nature, read Ephesians 4:23, 24 and Colossians 3:3-15.

• **2:15** Who are these spiritual rulers and authorities? Several suggestions have been made, including (1) demonic powers, (2) the gods of the powerful nations, (3) angels (highly regarded by the heretical teachers), or (4) the government of Rome. Since Paul did not identify who these rulers and authorities were, it could be any one of them, or all four. What Christ "disarmed" on the cross was any embodiment of rebellion in the world—whether that be Satan and his demons, false idols of pagan religious, evil world governments, or even God's good angels when they become objects of worship (as in the Colossian heresy). This "disarming" occurred when Jesus died on the cross, like stripping a defeated enemy of armor on the battlefield. Evil no longer has any power over believers because Christ has disarmed it. Paul already had told the Colossians, "He has rescued us from the kingdom of darkness and transferred us into the Kingdom of his dear Son" (1:13).

2:16 "What you eat or drink" probably refers to the Jewish dietary laws. The festivals mentioned are Jewish holy days celebrated annually, monthly (new moon), and weekly (the Sabbath). These rituals distinguished the Jews from their pagan neighbors. Failure to observe them could be easily noticed by those who were keeping track of what others did. But we should not let ourselves be judged by the opinions of others because Christ has set us free.

• **2:16, 17** Paul told the Colossian Christians not to let others criticize their diet or their religious ceremonies. Instead of outward observance, believers should focus on faith in Christ alone. Our worship, traditions, and ceremonies can help bring us close to God, but we should never criticize fellow Christians whose traditions and ceremonies differ from ours. More important than how we worship is that we worship Christ. Don't let anyone judge you. You are responsible to Christ.

2:17 Old Testament laws, holidays, and festivals pointed toward Christ. Paul calls them "shadows" of the reality that was to come—Christ himself. When Christ came, he dispelled the shadows. If we have Christ, we have what we need to know and please God.

2:17
Heb 8:5; 10:1

2:19
Eph 1:22;
4:15-16

2:20
Rom 6:6
Gal 4:3, 9

2:22
1 Cor 6:13

2:23
1 Tim 4:3

the reality yet to come. And Christ himself is that reality. [18]Don't let anyone condemn you by insisting on pious self-denial or the worship of angels,* saying they have had visions about these things. Their sinful minds have made them proud, [19]and they are not connected to Christ, the head of the body. For he holds the whole body together with its joints and ligaments, and it grows as God nourishes it.

[20]You have died with Christ, and he has set you free from the spiritual powers of this world. So why do you keep on following the rules of the world, such as, [21]"Don't handle! Don't taste! Don't touch!"? [22]Such rules are mere human teachings about things that deteriorate as we use them. [23]These rules may seem wise because they require strong devotion, pious self-denial, and severe bodily discipline. But they provide no help in conquering a person's evil desires.

2:18 Or *or worshiping with angels.*

FROM DEATH TO LIFE
What happens when we accept Christ

The Bible uses many illustrations to teach what happens when we choose to let Jesus be Lord of our lives. Following are some of the most vivid pictures:

1. Because Christ died for us, we have been crucified with him.	Romans 6:2-13; 7:4-6 2 Corinthians 5:14 Galatians 2:20; 5:24; 6:14 Colossians 2:20; 3:3-5 1 Peter 2:24
2. Our old, rebellious nature died with Christ.	Romans 6:6; 7:4-6 Colossians 3:9, 10
3. Christ's resurrection guarantees our new life now and eternal life with him later.	Romans 6:4, 11 Colossians 2:12, 13; 3:1, 3

This process is acted out in baptism (Colossians 2:12), based on our faith in Christ: (1) The old sinful nature dies (crucified). (2) We are ready to receive a new life (buried). (3) Christ gives us new life (resurrected).

2:18 The false teachers were claiming that God was far away and could be approached only through various levels of angels. They taught that people had to worship angels in order, eventually, to reach God. This is unscriptural; the Bible teaches that angels are God's servants, and it forbids worshiping them (Exodus 20:3, 4; Revelation 22:8, 9). As you grow in your Christian faith, let God's Word be your guide, not the opinions of other people.

● **2:19** The fundamental problem with the false teachers was that they were not connected to Christ, the head of the body of believers. If they had been joined to him, they could not have taught false doctrine or lived immorally. Anyone who teaches about God without being connected to him by faith should not be trusted.

2:20 The "rules of the world" are the beliefs of pagans. See 2:8 for more on Paul's view of non-Christian philosophy.

2:20; 3:1 How do we die with Christ, and how are we raised with him? When a person becomes a Christian, he or she is given new life through the power of the Holy Spirit. See the notes on 2:11, 12 and 2:13-15 for further information.

● **2:20-23** People should be able to see a difference between the way Christians and non-Christians live. Still, we should not expect instant maturity in new Christians. Christian growth is a lifelong process. Although we have a new nature, we don't automatically think all good thoughts and have all pure attitudes when we become new people in Christ. But if we keep listening to God, we will be changing all the time. As you look over the last year, what changes for the better have you seen in your thoughts and attitudes? Change may be slow, but your life will change significantly if you trust God to change you.

2:20-23 We cannot reach up to God by following rules of pious self-denial, by observing rituals, or by practicing religion. Paul isn't saying all rules are bad (see the note on Galatians 2:15, 16). But keeping laws or rules will not earn salvation. The Good News

is that God reaches down to human beings, and he asks for our response. Man-made religions focus on human effort; Christianity focuses on Christ's work. Believers must put aside sinful desires, but doing so is the by-product of our new life in Christ, not the reason for our new life. Our salvation does not depend on our own discipline and rule keeping but on the power of Christ's death and resurrection.

● **2:22, 23** We can guard against man-made religions by asking these questions about any religious group: (1) Does it stress man-made rules and taboos rather than God's grace? (2) Does it foster a critical spirit toward others, or does it exercise discipline discreetly and lovingly? (3) Does it stress formulas, secret knowledge, or special visions more than the Word of God? (4) Does it elevate self-righteousness, honoring those who keep the rules, rather than elevating Christ? (5) Does it neglect Christ's universal church, claiming to be an elite group? (6) Does it teach humiliation of the body as a means to spiritual growth rather than focus on the growth of the whole person? (7) Does it disregard the family rather than hold it in high regard as the Bible does?

● **2:23** To the Colossians, the discipline demanded by the false teachers seemed good, and legalism still attracts many people today. Following a long list of religious rules requires strong self-discipline and can make a person appear moral, but religious rules cannot change a person's heart. Only the Holy Spirit can do that.

2. What Christians should do
Living the New Life

3 Since you have been raised to new life with Christ, set your sights on the realities of heaven, where Christ sits in the place of honor at God's right hand. ²Think about the things of heaven, not the things of earth. ³For you died to this life, and your real life is hidden with Christ in God. ⁴And when Christ, who is your* life, is revealed to the whole world, you will share in all his glory.

⁵So put to death the sinful, earthly things lurking within you. Have nothing to do with sexual immorality, impurity, lust, and evil desires. Don't be greedy, for a greedy person is an idolater, worshiping the things of this world. ⁶Because of these sins, the anger of God is coming.* ⁷You used to do these things when your life was still part of this world. ⁸But now is the time to get rid of anger, rage, malicious behavior, slander, and dirty language. ⁹Don't lie to each other, for you have stripped off your old sinful nature and all its wicked deeds. ¹⁰Put on your new nature, and be renewed as you learn to know your Creator and become like him. ¹¹In this new life, it doesn't matter if you are a Jew or a Gentile,* circumcised or uncircumcised, barbaric, uncivilized,* slave, or free. Christ is all that matters, and he lives in all of us.

3:1 Matt 6:33 Eph 2:6
3:3 Rom 6:2 2 Cor 5:14
3:5 Rom 6:6; 8:13 Gal 5:19-21 Eph 4:19; 5:3, 5
3:7 Eph 2:2
3:8 Eph 4:25-31; 5:4
3:9 Eph 4:25
3:10 Rom 12:2 Eph 2:10; 4:24
3:11 Rom 10:12 1 Cor 12:13 Gal 3:28

3:4 Some manuscripts read *our.* **3:6** Some manuscripts read *is coming on all who disobey him.* **3:11a** Greek *a Greek.* **3:11b** Greek *Barbarian, Scythian.*

• **3:1ff** In chapter 2, Paul exposed the wrong reasons for self-denial. In chapter 3, he explains true Christian behavior—putting on the new nature by accepting Christ and regarding the earthly nature as dead. We change our moral and ethical behavior by letting Christ live within us, so that he can shape us into what we *should* be.

3:1, 2 Setting our sights on the realities of heaven means striving to put heaven's priorities into daily practice. Letting heaven fill our thoughts means concentrating on the eternal rather than the temporal. See Philippians 4:7 and Colossians 3:15 for more on Christ's rule in our hearts and minds.

• **3:2, 3** "For you died to this life" means that we should have as little desire for improper worldly pleasures as a dead person would have. The Christian's real home is where Christ lives (John 14:2, 3). This truth provides a different perspective on our lives here on earth. To "think about the things of heaven" means to look at life from God's perspective and to seek what he desires. This provides the antidote to materialism; we gain the proper perspective on material goods when we take God's view of them. It also provides the antidote to sensuality. By seeking what Christ desires, we have the power to break our obsession with pleasure and leisure activities. But it also provides the antidote to empty religiosity because following Christ means loving and serving in this world. Regard the world around you as God does; then you will live in harmony with him.

3:3 What does it mean that a believer's life is "hidden with Christ"? *Hidden* means "concealed and safe." This is not only a future hope but an accomplished fact right now. Our service and conduct do not earn our salvation, but they are results of our salvation. Take heart that your salvation is sure, and live each day for Christ.

• **3:4** Christ gives us power to live for him now, and he gives us hope for the future—he will return. In the rest of this chapter Paul explains how Christians should act *now* in order to be prepared for Christ's return.

3:5 We should consider ourselves dead and unresponsive to sexual immorality, impurity, lust, and evil desires. The warning in this verse is not against sex, but against sexual perversion. Where is the line between the two?

The Bible everywhere celebrates heterosexual, monogamous marriage as the proper situation for sexual fulfillment. Christian men and women should be open to true love—and to sexual intimacy—within the commitment to lifelong fidelity. That is God's way. The rest is dangerous and futile. Stay away. Sexual sin and perversion will drain your energies and turn your heart away from God.

3:6 "The anger of God" refers to God's judgment on these kinds of behavior, culminating with future and final punishment of evil. When tempted to sin, remember that you must one day stand before God.

• **3:8-10** We must rid ourselves of all evil practices and immorality. Then we can commit ourselves to what Christ teaches. Paul was urging the believers to remain true to their confession of faith. They were to rid themselves of the old life and put on the new nature given by Christ. If you have made such a commitment to Christ, are you remaining true to it?

3:9 Lying to one another disrupts unity by destroying trust. It tears down relationships and may lead to serious conflict in a church. So don't exaggerate statistics, pass on rumors and gossip, or say things to build up your own image. Be committed to telling the truth.

Jesus wants to clean your life and your church of sexual sin and verbal sin. There is no place in the Kingdom of God for hedonistic sexual experimentation or for gossip, rage, and backbiting. In their place, witness to the world like a lighthouse on a stormy night by displaying love, faith, and hope.

3:10 What does it mean to put on your new nature? It means that your conduct should match your faith. If you are a Christian, you should act like it. To be a Christian means more than just making good resolutions and having good intentions; it means taking the right actions. This is a straightforward step that is as simple as putting on your clothes. You must rid yourself of all evil practices and immorality. Then you can commit yourself to what Christ teaches. If you have made such a commitment to Christ, are you remaining true to it? What old clothes do you need to strip off?

3:10 Every Christian is in a continuing education program. The more we know of Christ and his work, the more we are being changed to be like him. Because this process is lifelong, we must never stop learning and obeying. There is no justification for drifting along, but there is an incentive to find the rich treasures of growing in him. It takes practice, ongoing review, patience, and concentration to keep in line with his will.

3:11 The Christian church should have no barriers of nationality, race, educational level, social standing, wealth, gender, religion, or power. Christ breaks down all barriers and accepts all people who come to him. Nothing should keep us from telling others about Christ or accepting into our fellowship any and all believers (Ephesians 2:14, 15). Christians should be building bridges, not walls.

3:12
Eph 4:2, 32
1 Pet 1:2

3:13
Eph 4:32; 5:2

3:14
Rom 13:8

3:15
John 14:27
Eph 2:14-16
Phil 4:7

3:17
1 Cor 10:31
Eph 5:20

12Since God chose you to be the holy people he loves, you must clothe yourselves with tenderhearted mercy, kindness, humility, gentleness, and patience. 13Make allowance for each other's faults, and forgive anyone who offends you. Remember, the Lord forgave you, so you must forgive others. 14Above all, clothe yourselves with love, which binds us all together in perfect harmony. 15And let the peace that comes from Christ rule in your hearts. For as members of one body you are called to live in peace. And always be thankful.

16Let the message about Christ, in all its richness, fill your lives. Teach and counsel each other with all the wisdom he gives. Sing psalms and hymns and spiritual songs to God with thankful hearts. 17And whatever you do or say, do it as a representative of the Lord Jesus, giving thanks through him to God the Father.

SINS VS. SIGNS OF LOVE

Sins of Sexual Attitude and Behavior	*Sins of Speech*	*Signs of Love*
Sexual immorality	Anger/Rage	Mercy
Impurity	Malicious behavior	Kindness
Lust	Slander	Humility
Evil desires	Dirty language	Gentleness
Greed	Lying	Patience
		Forgiveness

In Colossians 3:5 Paul tells us to put to death the things found in list 1. In 3:8, 9 he tells us to rid ourselves of the things found in list 2. In 3:12, 13 we're told to clothe ourselves with the things found in list 3. List 1 deals with sins of sexual attitudes and behavior—they are particularly destructive because of what they do to destroy any group or church. List 2 deals with sins of speech—these are the relationship breakers. List 3 contains the relationship builders, which we are to express as members of Christ's body.

• **3:12-17** Paul offers a strategy to help us live for God day by day: (1) Imitate Christ's compassionate, forgiving attitude (3:12, 13); (2) let love guide your life (3:14); (3) let the peace of Christ rule in your heart (3:15); (4) always be thankful (3:15); (5) keep God's Word in you at all times (3:16); (6) live as Jesus Christ's representative (3:17).

3:13 The key to forgiving others is remembering how much God has forgiven you. Is it difficult for you to forgive someone who has wronged you a little when God has forgiven you so much? Realizing God's infinite love and forgiveness can help you love and forgive others. Let God worry about the wrongs you've suffered. Don't quench your life in bitter feuding; live renewed in love and joy.

3:14 All the virtues that Paul encourages us to develop are perfectly bound together by love. As we clothe ourselves with these virtues, the last garment we are to put on is love, which holds all of the others in place. To practice any list of virtues without practicing love will lead to distortion, fragmentation, and stagnation (1 Corinthians 13:3).

• **3:14, 15** Christians should live in peace. To live in peace does not mean that suddenly all differences of opinion are eliminated, but it does require that loving Christians work together despite their differences. Such love is not a feeling but a decision to meet others' needs (see 1 Corinthians 13). To clothe ourselves with love leads to peace between individuals and among the members of the body of believers. Do problems in your relationships with other Christians cause open conflicts or mutual silence? Consider what you can do to heal those relationships with love.

3:15 The word *rule* comes from the language of athletics: Paul tells us to let Christ's peace be umpire or referee in our heart. Our heart is the center of conflict because there our feelings and desires clash—our fears and hopes, distrust and trust, jealousy and love. How can we deal with these constant conflicts and live as God wants? Paul explains that we must decide between conflicting elements by using the rule of peace. Which choice will promote peace in our souls and in our churches? For more on the peace of Christ, see Philippians 4:7.

• **3:16** Although the early Christians had access to the Old Testament and freely used it, they did not yet have the New Testament or any other Christian books to study. Their stories and teachings about Christ were memorized and passed on from person to person. Sometimes the teachings were set to music, and so music became an important part of Christian worship and education.

3:16 Thankful people can worship wholeheartedly. Gratitude opens our hearts to God's peace and enables us to put on love. Discontented people constantly calculate what's wrong with their lot in life.

To increase your thankfulness, take an inventory of all you have (including your relationships, memories, abilities, and family, as well as material possessions). Use the inventory for prayers of gratitude. On Sunday, before worship, quit rushing around; instead, take time to reflect on reasons for thanks. Declare Sunday as your "thanks, faith, and hope" day. Celebrate God's goodness to you, and ask in prayer for all your needs for the week ahead.

• **3:17** "Whatever you do or say, do it as a representative of the Lord Jesus" means bringing honor to Christ in every aspect and activity of daily living. As a Christian, you represent Christ at all times—wherever you go and whatever you say. What impression do people have of Christ when they see or talk with you? What changes would you make in your life in order to honor Christ?

Instructions for Christian Households

18Wives, submit to your husbands, as is fitting for those who belong to the Lord.

19Husbands, love your wives and never treat them harshly.

20Children, always obey your parents, for this pleases the Lord. 21Fathers, do not aggravate your children, or they will become discouraged.

22Slaves, obey your earthly masters in everything you do. Try to please them all the time, not just when they are watching you. Serve them sincerely because of your reverent fear of the Lord. 23Work willingly at whatever you do, as though you were working for the Lord rather than for people. 24Remember that the Lord will give you an inheritance as your reward, and that the Master you are serving is Christ.* 25But if you do what is wrong, you will be paid back for the wrong you have done. For God has no favorites.

4 Masters, be just and fair to your slaves. Remember that you also have a Master— in heaven.

An Encouragement for Prayer

2Devote yourselves to prayer with an alert mind and a thankful heart. 3Pray for us, too, that God will give us many opportunities to speak about his mysterious plan concerning Christ. That is why I am here in chains. 4Pray that I will proclaim this message as clearly as I should.

3:18 Eph 5:22
3:19 Eph 5:25 1 Pet 3:7
3:20 Eph 6:1
3:21-25 //Eph 6:4-8
3:25 Acts 10:34
4:1 Lev 25:43 Eph 6:9
4:2 Luke 18:1 Eph 6:18 1 Thes 5:17
4:4 Eph 6:20

3:24 Or *and serve Christ as your Master.*

• **3:18–4:1** Paul gives rules for three sets of household relationships: (1) husbands and wives, (2) parents and children, and (3) slave owners and slaves. In each case there is mutual responsibility to submit and love, to obey and encourage, to work hard and be fair. Examine your family and work relationships. Do you relate to others as God intended? See Ephesians 5:21–6:9 for similar instructions.

3:18, 19 Why is submission of wives to husbands "fitting for those who belong to the Lord"? This may have been good advice for Christian women, newly freed in Christ, who found submission difficult. Paul told them that they should willingly follow their husbands' leadership in Christ. But Paul had words for husbands as well: "Husbands, love your wives and never treat them harshly." It may also have been true that Christian men, used to the Roman custom of giving unlimited power to the head of the family, were not used to treating their wives with respect and love. Real spiritual leadership involves service. Just as Christ served the disciples, even to the point of washing their feet, so the husband is to serve his wife. This means putting aside his own interests in order to care for his wife. A wise and Christ-honoring husband will not abuse his leadership role. At the same time, a wise and Christ-honoring wife will not try to undermine her husband's leadership. Either approach causes disunity and friction in marriage. For more on submission, see the notes on Ephesians 5:21-33.

3:20, 21 Children must be handled with care. They need firm discipline administered in love. Parents should not aggravate them by nagging, deriding, or destroying their self-respect so that they quit trying.

However, the opposite problem occurs when parents are afraid to correct a child for fear of stifling some aspect of his or her personality or losing his or her love. Single parents or parents who cannot spend much time with a child may be prone to indulgence. But such children, especially, need the security of guidance and structure. Boundaries and guidelines will not embitter a child. Instead, they will set the child free to live securely within the boundaries.

• **3:22–4:1** Paul does not condemn or condone slavery but explains that Christ transcends all divisions between people.

Slaves are told to work hard as though their owner were Christ himself (3:23); but owners should be just and fair (4:1). Perhaps Paul was thinking specifically of Onesimus and Philemon—the slave and master whose conflict lay behind the letter to Philemon (see the book of Philemon). Philemon was a slave owner in the Colossian church, and Onesimus had been his slave (4:9).

3:23 Since the Creation, God has given us work to do. If we could regard our work as an act of worship or service to God, such an attitude would take some of the drudgery and boredom out of it. We could work without complaining or resentment if we would treat our job problems as the cost of discipleship.

4:1 Slave owners were to provide what was just and fair. Similarly today, employers should pay fair wages and treat their employees justly. Paul's instructions encourage responsibility and integrity on the job. Christian employees should do their jobs as if Jesus Christ were their supervisor. And Christian employers should treat their employees fairly and with respect. Can you be trusted to do your best, even when the boss is not around? Do you work hard and with enthusiasm? Do you treat your employees as people, not machines? Employers should pay fair wages and treat their employees justly. Leaders should take care of their volunteers and not abuse them. If you have responsibility over others, make sure you do what is just and fair. Remember that no matter whom you work for, and no matter who works for you, the One you ultimately should want to please is your Father in heaven. You are accountable to him.

• **4:2** Have you ever grown tired of praying for something or someone? Paul says we should "devote" ourselves to prayer and be "alert" in prayer. Our persistence is an expression of our faith that God answers our prayers. Faith shouldn't die if the answers come slowly, for the delay may be God's way of working his will in our life. When you feel tired of praying, know that God is present, always listening, always answering—maybe not in ways you had hoped, but in ways that he knows are best.

4:3 The "mysterious plan" is Christ's Good News of salvation. The whole focus of Paul's life was to tell others about Christ, explaining and preaching this wonderful mystery.

4:4 Paul asked for prayer that he could proclaim the Good News about Christ clearly, and we can request prayer to do the same. No matter what approach to evangelism we use, whether emphasizing lifestyle and example or whether building relationships, we should never obscure the message of the Good News.

4:5
Eph 5:15-16
4:6
Eph 4:29
1 Pet 3:15

4:7-8
Acts 20:4
Eph 6:21-22
4:9
Phlm 1:10

4:10
Acts 12:12; 15:37;
19:29; 20:4; 27:2

4:12
Col 1:7
Phlm 1:23
4:13
Col 2:1
4:14
2 Tim 4:10-11
Phlm 1:24
4:15
Rom 16:5

⁵Live wisely among those who are not believers, and make the most of every opportunity. ⁶Let your conversation be gracious and attractive* so that you will have the right response for everyone.

Paul's Final Instructions and Greetings

⁷Tychicus will give you a full report about how I am getting along. He is a beloved brother and faithful helper who serves with me in the Lord's work. ⁸I have sent him to you for this very purpose—to let you know how we are doing and to encourage you. ⁹I am also sending Onesimus, a faithful and beloved brother, one of your own people. He and Tychicus will tell you everything that's happening here.

¹⁰Aristarchus, who is in prison with me, sends you his greetings, and so does Mark, Barnabas's cousin. As you were instructed before, make Mark welcome if he comes your way. ¹¹Jesus (the one we call Justus) also sends his greetings. These are the only Jewish believers among my co-workers; they are working with me here for the Kingdom of God. And what a comfort they have been!

¹²Epaphras, a member of your own fellowship and a servant of Christ Jesus, sends you his greetings. He always prays earnestly for you, asking God to make you strong and perfect, fully confident that you are following the whole will of God. ¹³I can assure you that he prays hard for you and also for the believers in Laodicea and Hierapolis.

¹⁴Luke, the beloved doctor, sends his greetings, and so does Demas. ¹⁵Please give my greetings to our brothers and sisters* at Laodicea, and to Nympha and the church that meets in her house.

4:6 Greek *and seasoned with salt.*   **4:15** Greek *brothers.*

RULES OF SUBMISSION

Wives, submit to your husbands (3:18).

Children, always obey your parents (3:20).

Slaves, obey your earthly masters (3:22).

(*Employees,* work hard for your employers.)

Husbands, love your wives and never treat them harshly (3:19).

Fathers, do not aggravate your children, or they will become discouraged (3:21).

Masters, be just and fair to your slaves (4:1).

(*Employers,* be just and fair with your employees.)

The New Testament includes many instructions concerning relationships. Most people read these instructions for the other person and ignore the ones that apply to themselves. But you can't control another person's behavior, only your own. Start by following your own instructions and not insisting on the obedience of others first.

4:5 We should be wise in our contacts with non-believers, making the most of our opportunities to tell them the Good News of salvation. What opportunities do you have?

• **4:6** When we tell others about Christ, it is important always to be gracious in what we say. No matter how much sense the message makes, we lose our effectiveness if we are not courteous. Just as we like to be respected, we must respect others if we want them to listen to what we have to say.

• **4:7** Tychicus was one of Paul's personal representatives and probably the bearer of the letters to the Colossians and Ephesians (see also Ephesians 6:21, 22). He accompanied Paul to Jerusalem with the collection for the church (Acts 20:4).

• **4:10** Aristarchus was a Thessalonian who accompanied Paul on his third missionary journey. He was with Paul in the riot at Ephesus (Acts 19:29). He and Tychicus were with Paul in Greece (Acts 20:4). Aristarchus went to Rome (Acts 27:2). Mark started out with Paul and Barnabas on their first missionary journey (Acts 12:25), but he left in the middle of the trip for unknown reasons (Acts 13:13). Barnabas and Mark were relatives, and when Paul refused to take Mark on another journey, Barnabas and Mark journeyed together to preach the Good News (Acts 15:37-41). Mark also worked with Peter (Acts 12:12, 13; 1 Peter 5:13). Later, Mark and Paul were reconciled (Philemon 1:24). Mark wrote the Gospel of Mark. His Profile is in Acts 13, p. 1847.

• **4:12** Epaphras founded the Colossian church (see the note on 1:7), and his report to Paul in Rome caused Paul to write this letter. Epaphras was a hero of the Colossian church, one of the believers who helped keep the church together despite growing troubles. His earnest prayers for the believers show his deep love and concern for them.

4:13 Laodicea was located a few miles northwest of Colosse; Hierapolis was about five miles north of Laodicea. See the note on 2:1 for more about Laodicea.

• **4:14** Luke spent much time with Paul, not only accompanying him on most of his third missionary journey but sitting with him in the prison at Rome. Luke wrote the Gospel of Luke and the book of Acts. His Profile is in Acts 17, p. 1865. Demas was faithful for a while, but then he deserted Paul because he loved "the things of this life" (2 Timothy 4:10).

• **4:15** The early Christians often met in homes. Church buildings were not common until the third century.

16After you have read this letter, pass it on to the church at Laodicea so they can read it, too. And you should read the letter I wrote to them.

17And say to Archippus, "Be sure to carry out the ministry the Lord gave you."

18HERE IS MY GREETING IN MY OWN HANDWRITING—PAUL.

Remember my chains.

May God's grace be with you.

4:16
1 Thes 5:27
2 Thes 3:14

4:17
2 Tim 4:5
Phlm 1:2

4:18
1 Cor 16:21
2 Thes 3:17

4:16 Some suggest that the letter from Laodicea may be the book of Ephesians, because the letter to the Ephesians was circulated to all the churches in Asia Minor. It is also possible that there was a special letter to the Laodiceans, of which we have no record today. Paul wrote several letters that have been lost (see, for example, 2 Corinthians 2:3 and note).

4:17 Paul's letter to Philemon is also addressed to Archippus (Philemon 1:2). Paul called him a "fellow soldier." He may have been a Roman soldier who had become a member of the Colossian church, or he may have been Philemon's son.

4:17 Paul encouraged Archippus to make sure that he carried out the ministry he had received in the Lord. There are many ways for us to leave our ministries unfinished. We can easily get sidetracked morally, we can become exhausted and stop, we can get mad and quit, or we can let it slide and leave it up to others. We should see to it that we finish God's assignments, completing the work we have received.

• **4:18** Paul usually dictated his letters to a secretary and then often ended with a short note in his own handwriting (see also 1 Corinthians 16:21; Galatians 6:11). This assured the recipients that false teachers were not writing letters in Paul's name. It also gave the letters a personal touch.

• **4:18** To understand the letter to the Colossians, we need to know that the church was facing pressure from a heresy that promised deeper spiritual life through secret knowledge (an early form of Gnosticism). The false teachers were destroying faith in Christ by undermining Christ's humanity and divinity.

Paul makes it clear in Colossians that Christ alone is the source of our spiritual life, the head of the body of believers. Christ is Lord of both the physical and spiritual worlds. The path to deeper spiritual life is not through religious duties, special knowledge, or secrets; it is only through a clear connection with the Lord Jesus Christ. We must never let anything come between us and our Savior.

STUDY QUESTIONS

Thirteen lessons for individual or group study

HOW TO USE THIS BIBLE STUDY

It's always exciting to get more than you expect. And that's what you'll find in this Bible study guide—much more than you expect. Our goal was to write thoughtful, practical, dependable, and application-oriented studies of God's word.

This study guide contains the complete text of the selected Bible book. The commentary is accurate, complete, and loaded with unique charts, maps, and profiles of Bible people.

With the Bible text, extensive notes and features, and questions to guide discussion, Life Application Bible Studies have everything you need in one place.

The lessons in this Bible study guide will work for large classes as well as small-group studies. To get everyone involved in your discussions, encourage participants to answer the questions before each meeting.

Each lesson is divided into five easy-to-lead sections. The section called "Reflect" introduces you and the members of your group to a specific area of life touched by the lesson. "Read" shows which chapters to read and which notes and other features to use. Additional questions help you understand the passage. "Realize" brings into focus the biblical principle to be learned with questions, a special insight, or both. "Respond" helps you make connections with your own situation and personal needs. The questions are designed to help you find areas in your life where you can apply the biblical truths. "Resolve" helps you map out action plans for that day.

Begin and end each lesson with prayer, asking for the Holy Spirit's guidance, direction, and wisdom.

Recommended time allotments for each section of a lesson are as follows:

Segment	60 minutes	90 minutes
Reflect on your life	*5 minutes*	*10 minutes*
Read the passage	*10 minutes*	*15 minutes*
Realize the principle	*15 minutes*	*20 minutes*
Respond to the message	*20 minutes*	*30 minutes*
Resolve to take action	*10 minutes*	*15 minutes*

All five sections work together to help a person learn the lessons, live out the principles, and obey the commands taught in the Bible.

Also, at the end of each lesson, there is a section entitled "More for studying other themes in this section." These questions will help you lead the group in studying other parts of each section not covered in depth by the main lesson.

But don't just listen to God's word. You must do what it says. Otherwise, you are only fooling yourselves. For if you listen to the word and don't obey, it is like glancing at your face in a mirror. You see yourself, walk away, and forget what you look like. But if you look carefully into the perfect law that sets you free, and if you do what it says and don't forget what you heard, then God will bless you for doing it (James 1:22-25).

LESSON 1
PARTNERS
PHILIPPIANS 1:1-11

REFLECT
on your life

1 Think of your closest friends. Why are you thankful for each one?

_____

_____

_____

_____

READ
the passage

Read the introductory material to Philippians, 1:1-11, and the following notes:

❐ 1:1   ❐ 1:4   ❐ 1:4, 5   ❐ 1:6   ❐ 1:7   ❐ 1:7, 8   ❐ 1:10

2 Describe Paul's special relationship with the believers at Philippi. How did this relationship develop?

_____

_____

_____

3 What is the "good work" that was begun in these believers?

_____

_____

_____

4 How do love and knowledge work together to produce growth in the life of a believer?

_____

_____

_____

5 Describe the different partnerships mentioned or implied in this section.

_____

_____

_____

_____

_____

REALIZE
the principle

Partnership summarizes an important facet of Paul's view of the church. Paul was filled with joy as he thought about those who prayed for, encouraged, and supported him in Philippi. He had helped them just a few years earlier, and now they were helping him. It was a two-way relationship—there was mutual love and support. Partnership should characterize the church today. In fact, this is what it means to function as the body of Christ, helping and supporting your church and other believers you know.

6 What can a local congregation do to promote and nurture supportive relationships within the church?

_____

_____

_____

_____

7 How can your church partner with believers from other congregations?

_____

_____

_____

_____

_____

8 Reflect on your growth in faith over the years. Who encouraged you most and brought out the best in you? How did they do this?

RESPOND
to the message

_____

_____

_____

_____

9 Whom might you be able to encourage and support? Which of that person's needs might you be able to meet?

_____

_____

_____

_____

10 What are you doing to further caring relationships in your church or among your circle of friends? What opportunities do you have to do this?

_____

_____

_____

_____

_____

RESOLVE
to take action

11 Name at least one person who has helped you grow as a Christian, and then thank him or her for that encouragement in a visit, phone call, or letter.

_____

_____

_____

_____

12 Identify someone around you who needs encouragement today. Ask God to help you understand his or her circumstances and needs. What can you do to show you care and want to help that person grow?

_____

_____

_____

_____

MORE
for studying
other themes
in this section

A Given Philippi's strategic location, what kind of city would you expect it to be? What unique resources and opportunities would be there? What typical problems and barriers for the church would you expect to find?

B What kinds of problems was the church in Philippi having? What did Paul advise? What similar kinds of problems do churches have today?

C How might the influence of Greek and Roman thought affect Paul's message and approach to the Philippian believers? How should our culture affect the way we communicate God's word?

D What do these opening verses suggest regarding Paul's personal circumstances and his attitude toward them?

E Why was Timothy with Paul at this time?

F To whom was the greeting "to all of God's holy people" (1:1) directed? What does this suggest about the nature of the church? What were the roles and responsibilities of the elders and deacons in the early church?

G What fruit of salvation (1:11) should we expect to see in our life? How does the cultivation of this fruit depend on Jesus?

H What gives us happiness? What robs us of happiness? What gives us joy?

LESSON 2
DEFEATING DISCOURAGEMENT
PHILIPPIANS 1:12-26

R
REFLECT
on your life

1 Describe a time of deep discouragement in your life. What caused your discouragement, and how did you snap out of it?

_____

_____

_____

_____

_____

R
READ
the passage

Read Philippians 1:12-26 and the following notes:

❏ 1:12-14   ❏ 1:13   ❏ 1:15-18   ❏ 1:19-21   ❏ 1:20, 21

2 How did Paul respond to his misfortunes?

_____

_____

_____

3 Why did Paul seem so unconcerned about the motives of those who were preaching Christ for the wrong reasons?

_____

_____

_____

_____

4 How could Paul be so unconcerned about death?

_____

_____

_____

_____

5 Why was Paul so confident of vindication and release?

_____

_____

_____

_____

_____

6 What might have caused Paul to be ashamed?

_____

_____

_____

_____

Paul had plenty of reasons for becoming discouraged—he faced imprisonment, bitter rivalries, and personal setbacks. Yet he could face the future
with confidence because he was not living for himself. Instead of trying to
feel good and be successful, Paul lived to serve the Lord and to help others.
Because Paul's life centered around his walk with God, circumstances became
irrelevant, others' motives and actions couldn't discourage him, and personal
uncertainty could not render him powerless. We can have this same peace
and confidence by putting Christ at the center of all we do. He will lift us above
our circumstances and enable us to face our challenges, knowing that everything is in his hands.

REALIZE
the principle

7 In a discouraging situation, what can a person choose to do?

_____

_____

_____

_____

8 How do you usually react to tough times? What might help you to become more positive in your attitudes and responses?

_____

_____

_____

_____

_____

9 How can difficult circumstances increase your dependence on Christ?

_____

_____

_____

_____

10 In what circumstances or with which people do you easily become discouraged?

_____

_____

_____

11 What can you do to guard against these discouraging influences?

_____

_____

_____

_____

12 Select one aspect of your life that is most discouraging to you. What is making you feel discouraged? How could you react differently? What attitude change might you make?

_____

_____

_____

_____

MORE
for studying
other themes
in this section

A What does the freedom of Paul's house arrest suggest about the Roman view of Christianity at that time? How did God use Paul's imprisonment to spread the gospel?

B In Paul's day, why might some Christians have been happy at the thought of Paul in prison and perhaps even wish to cause him further difficulty? Why do believers sometimes act this way?

C Whom do you know whose life is focused on Christ? How do they maintain this focus? In what ways would you like to be more like them?

D What makes it difficult for us to keep our faith in Christ? Why do we find it difficult to witness boldly for Christ? What can you do to be a stronger witness for Christ?

E In which situations do you need to speak the word of God more courageously? What barriers make this difficult, and what can you do to overcome them?

F In what areas of your Christian life are you doing the right actions for the wrong reasons? What should you do to correct this?

G How should we handle a situation where someone is involved in Christian work or ministry for the wrong reasons?

LESSON 3
UNITED WITH A CAUSE
PHILIPPIANS 1:27–2:11

REFLECT
on your life

1 List two or three examples of people who have become united for an important cause.

_____

_____

_____

_____

2 What has been the most unified team of which you have been a part? What built the unity?

_____

_____

_____

_____

READ
the passage

Read Philippians 1:27–2:11 and the following notes:

❐ 1:29 ❐ 1:30 ❐ 2:1-5 ❐ 2:3 ❐ 2:4 ❐ 2:5-11

3 In a cosmopolitan city like Philippi, what differences among believers could have made it difficult to preserve unity in the church?

_____

_____

_____

_____

4 What external opposition might the Philippian church have been facing?

_____

_____

_____

5 Why would the fearlessness of Christians be taken as "a sign" (a bad omen) by their opponents?

_____

_____

_____

6 What does 2:5-11 tell us about who Christ is and what he did?

_____

_____

_____

7 What essential characteristics of Christ's attitude does Paul challenge us to have?

_____

REALIZE
the principle

_____

_____

Paul challenges the church at Philippi to be unified for the cause of Christ, refusing to act out of self-centeredness or pride. This unity would come if each believer followed the example of Christ, who gave up everything to die for them. Christlike humility is the key to unity. The more we are committed to Christ and to living like him, the more we will be committed to each other. As a result, we will be able to face opposition and hardship, and we will be able to advance the cause of Christ in the world.

8 What might be the consequences, both good and bad, of a person's neglecting his or her own needs and concentrating instead on meeting the needs of others?

_____

_____

_____

_____

9 Why should unity be an important goal for any church?

_____

_____

_____

_____

RESPOND
to the message

10 What influences in our culture reinforce our attitudes of self-importance and self-interest? What can the church do to counter these?

_____

_____

_____

_____

_____

11 What are potentially the most divisive issues facing your church? What could you do to help resolve those internal tensions?

_____

_____

_____

_____

12 How do you explain the apparent lack of sacrifice, suffering, and service in many churches today? What can believers do to change this situation?

_____

_____

_____

_____

13 Which causes unify your church? For which causes would you like to see your church unified in the future?

_____

_____

_____

14 What barriers to unity have you noticed in your church?

_____

_____

_____

_____

15 What steps can you take to help unify your church? Who might be able
to help you in this process?

_____

_____

_____

_____

RESOLVE
to take action

A Paul uses the phrase "fighting together" from Greek athletic games to
describe how Christians should work together. Why is this an appropriate
description?

MORE
for studying
other themes
in this section

B What are the most common forms of opposition facing the church today?
How well is the church responding?

C What did Christ give up to become a human? What is the significance
of Jesus' dying a criminal's death on the cross?

D At the final judgment, what will be the experience of those who have rejected
Christ?

E If you need to make a sacrifice to be closer to Christ, what might you have
to give up? What is stopping you from making that sacrifice? What does this
suggest about your values?

LESSON 4
LIGHT IN DARKNESS
PHILIPPIANS 2:12-30

REFLECT
on your life

1 List some of the shining stars of the faith today. Why do they stand out from the crowd? In what ways do you wish you were more like them?

_____

_____

_____

_____

_____

READ
the passage

Read Philippians 2:12-30, the chart "Three Stages of Perfection," and the following notes:

❐ 2:12   ❐ 2:13   ❐ 2:14-16   ❐ 2:17   ❐ 2:19, 22   ❐ 2:23   ❐ 2:25

2 What examples of crookedness and perversity might we have expected to find in Philippi at the time of this letter?

_____

_____

_____

_____

3 What do we know about Timothy and his relationship with Paul? How had Timothy proved himself as a servant of Christ?

_____

_____

_____

_____

4 In what ways had Epaphroditus proven himself?

_____

_____

_____

5 What does it take to become a Christian who shines out in the world?

_____

_____

_____

_____

REALIZE
the principle

Paul encourages the Philippian believers to let their lives shine brightly (2:15) in a dark world. Then he mentions Timothy and Epaphroditus as outstanding examples. When people give themselves fully to the Lord's service, there is something unavoidably attractive about them. They stand out like beacons of light in a dark sky. Jesus said we are "the light of the world" (Matthew 5:14). How brightly do you shine?

6 How do complaining and arguing dim our light?

_____

_____

_____

7 Read the chart "Three Stages of Perfection" and summarize each stage.

a. *Perfect Relationship.* What does this mean? What has Christ done or what will he do? What must we do? _____

RESPOND
to the message

_____

_____

b. *Perfect Progress.* What does this mean? What has Christ done or what will he do? What must we do?_____

_____

_____

c. *Completely Perfect.* What does this mean? What has Christ done or what will he do? What must we do? _____

_____

_____

8 What prevents you from becoming a shining example of a Christian? What external barriers hinder you? What internal barriers must you overcome?

_____

_____

_____

_____

_____

9 How should we honor those who exhibit fine character and attain the high standards of servant leadership? What would probably be most meaningful to them?

_____

_____

_____

_____

_____

10 In your church, who is most effective in discipling others toward effective Christian living? What can you learn from his or her approach to developing others?

_____

_____

_____

_____

_____

11 What steps can your church take to help exceptional servants reproduce themselves?

_____

_____

_____

_____

_____

12 Who in your own church is a good example of servanthood? How can you learn from that person?

_____

_____

_____

13 What character qualities of Timothy or Epaphroditus would you like to develop in your life?

_____

_____

_____

14 What dims or blocks your light from shining more brightly for Christ?

_____

_____

_____

_____

_____

RESOLVE
to take action

15 What can you do to brighten your light or remove the barrier? What could you ask God to do?

_____

_____

_____

A How can we put into action God's work in our life? What keeps this from being simply a form of works-based righteousness? What does the phrase "with deep reverence and fear" (2:12) mean in relation to how we ought to translate our faith into action?

MORE
for studying
other themes
in this section

B How do arguing and complaining hinder our spiritual growth?

C What does Paul mean when he describes himself as being poured out "like a liquid offering" (2:17)? How might you give your life for someone else?

D How is it possible to rejoice when we are suffering?

E What does it mean to "hold firmly to the word of life" (2:16)?

LESSON 5
PRESSING TOWARD THE GOAL
PHILIPPIANS 3:1–4:1

REFLECT
on your life

1 What is your favorite Summer Olympics event? Why?

_____

_____

_____

_____

2 What kind of training is necessary to become a world-class athlete?

_____

_____

_____

READ
the passage

Read Philippians 3:1–4:1, the chart "Training for the Christian Life," and the following notes:

❐ 3:2, 3   ❐ 3:4-6   ❐ 3:8   ❐ 3:10   ❐ 3:12-14   ❐ 3:13, 14   ❐ 3:17

❐ 3:17-21   ❐ 3:20

3 What was Paul's goal in life?

_____

_____

_____

4 What does Paul consider worthless in comparison with knowing Christ?

_____

_____

_____

5 What kind of behavior did Paul want to prevent among the believers?

_____

_____

_____

_____

6 What role does personal effort play in our Christian growth?

_____

_____

_____

_____

_____

REALIZE
the principle

Paul compares the Christian life with running a race. Just as athletes place themselves under strict training and compete with all of their might, so all believers should "press on to reach the end of the race" (3:14). This means that we must place ourselves under training, discipline our bodies and minds, and watch where we are going. This leaves no place for complacency, laziness, distractions, or moral slackness. Are you playing to win? Are you in training? Are you in the race? To what degree are you "press[ing] on to reach the end of the race" (3:14)?

7 In what ways is a race an appropriate metaphor for illustrating what it means to live for Christ?

_____

_____

_____

_____

8 Review the chart "Training for the Christian Life," and summarize your responsibilities in the process.

1 Corinthians 9:24-27

RESPOND
to the message

_____

_____

_____

Philippians 3:13, 14

_____

_____

_____

1 Timothy 4:7-10

_____

_____

_____

2 Timothy 4:7, 8

_____

_____

_____

9 Which of these areas of training is the easiest or most natural for you? Which demands the most effort, concentration, and discipline?

_____

_____

_____

10 What picture (athlete, soldier, etc.) is most meaningful to you in describing what is involved in "press[ing] on to reach the end of the race" (3:14) in your Christian growth? Why?

_____

_____

_____

_____

11 Paul considered all his past accomplishments worthless for the sake of Christ. How can our past accomplishments and honors sometimes get in the way of our growth in the Lord?

_____

_____

_____

_____

12 What does it mean to forget "the past" (3:13)? What does it mean to look "forward to what lies ahead" (3:13)? How do we "reach the end of the race" (3:14)?

_____

_____

_____

_____

13 In what ways do you need to get more serious about running the race of the Christian life? Identify one or two areas where you need to discipline yourself more effectively. What could you do to improve the effectiveness of your training?

RESOLVE
to take action

_____

_____

_____

_____

A Why would Paul's background have been a source of pride to him before he became a Christian? Why was he so willing to give it up for Christ? How can pride hinder our relationship with Christ?

MORE
for studying
other themes
in this section

B What does this passage tell us about the coming resurrection?

C How is the exhortation to rejoice in the Lord a safeguard for believers?

D In this passage, Paul is highly critical of two groups of so-called Christians: the Judaizers (see note on 3:2, 3) and the overindulgent (3:18, 19). How did they distort the gospel and thus distract sincere believers from knowing and applying its truth? What individuals or groups try to distract believers today? What should be done to correct these harmful teachings and practices?

E What does it mean to "put no confidence in human effort" (3:3)? Why is that important?

F Drawing from this whole chapter, what does Paul mean by the phrase "know Christ" (3:10)? What more is involved than simply believing in Jesus as God's Son?

G How does righteousness by faith set us free to grow in our knowledge of Christ and in his service?

H How can we keep the foundation of our past growth in Christ from crumbling away?

I Why do we sometimes fail to "hold on to the progress we have already made" (3:16)?

LESSON 6
AN ATTITUDE OF GRATITUDE
PHILIPPIANS 4:2-9

REFLECT
on your life

1 Finish this sentence: You know it's going to be a bad day when . . .

_____

_____

2 What would you say to help someone feel more optimistic about life?

_____

_____

READ
the passage

Read Philippians 4:2-9 and the following notes:

❐ 4:2, 3   ❐ 4:4   ❐ 4:6, 7   ❐ 4:7   ❐ 4:8

3 What does Paul recommend for all believers regarding prayer?

_____

_____

_____

4 What promises are recorded in this section?

_____

_____

_____

5 Why does Paul encourage believers to follow his example?

_____

_____

_____

6 How is being full of joy in the Lord different from trying to have a more positive outlook on life?

REALIZE
the principle

_____

_____

_____

_____

Philippians is described as a book filled with joy, and here (4:4) Paul encourages the Philippian believers to be full of joy. We may wonder how this is possible, especially considering the problems and pressures we face. But consider Paul. He gave up his security and status and endured an endless series of trials for the sake of his love for Christ. And writing this as a prisoner of Rome, he tells us to rejoice. What would it take to change you into a joyful Christian?

7 Why is it healthier to focus on what is excellent and worthy of praise rather than to concentrate on identifying problems? How can we learn from mistakes and bad examples and still focus on the positive?

_____

_____

_____

_____

_____

8 List an example you can focus on (a person, an event, or a thought) for each of the following categories:

RESPOND
to the message

True (genuine, not deceptive or illusory)

_____

Honorable (worthy, serious)

_____

Right (one's duty and responsibility to God and others)

_____

Pure (morally undefiled)

_____

Lovely (attractive, winsome)

_____

Admirable (worthy of esteem)

_____

Excellent (fulfilling one's God-given potential in every area of life)

_____

_____

Worthy of praise (that which God would commend)

_____

_____

9 Which are the easiest for you? Which are the most difficult? What could you do to think more about such things?

_____

_____

_____

_____

10 What causes a person to develop a negative attitude about life?

_____

_____

_____

11 What causes some people to approach life with an attitude of gratitude?

_____

_____

_____

12 What can we do to prevent our critical side from dominating how we see things?

_____

_____

_____

13 What can we do to control what we think about?

_____

_____

_____

14 Where do you need to make an attitude adjustment? Ask God to help you change your thoughts and outlook in this area.

_____

_____

_____

RESOLVE
to take action

A What is the "Book of Life" mentioned in 4:3? Whose names are in it, and how were they placed there?

B Paul seemed convinced that Jesus would return soon, and yet we are still awaiting his triumphant return. How should we act during this seeming delay in the fulfillment of the Lord's promise?

C Why was Paul so upset about the conflict between Euodia and Syntyche? Whom did he ask to intervene to help them resolve their differences? What conflicts are there in your church? How can you help resolve them?

D What are the most common causes of broken relationships? How should we respond to broken relationships between believers? What does the Bible say about the process of reconciliation? What responsibility do other Christians have for encouraging this process?

E How does prayer work? What are some common traps we fall into in our prayer life? How can we avoid these pitfalls?

MORE
for studying
other themes
in this section

LESSON 7
GIVERS AND GIFTS
PHILIPPIANS 4:10-23

REFLECT
on your life

1 Describe the most meaningful gift you have ever received.

_____

_____

_____

_____

READ
the passage

Read Philippians 4:10-23 and the following notes:

❏ 4:10   ❏ 4:10-14   ❏ 4:12, 13   ❏ 4:17   ❏ 4:18   ❏ 4:19   ❏ 4:22   ❏ 4:23

2 Describe the changes in Paul's financial condition throughout his life. How did he react to those changes?

_____

_____

_____

_____

3 What was Paul's attitude toward the gifts from the Philippian believers?

_____

_____

_____

_____

_____

4 What does the phrase "from his glorious riches" suggest concerning God's ability to meet our needs? What does it say about the process he uses?

_____

_____

_____

_____

5 What key principles of biblical stewardship are presented in this passage?

_____

_____

_____

_____

REALIZE
the principle

Paul took time to thank the Philippians for their generous gifts to him and the church at Jerusalem. And he explained how to be content in any circumstance. The Philippians were good examples of what it means to care for each other. God wants us to care for each other too, and to recognize that he is the one behind every gift. When we become too concerned about hanging on to what we have, we cannot be used to help others in need. When we are too ashamed to admit our own needs, we cannot be used to bless others who feel led to give. Only when we look at our life from God's perspective can we experience the complete joy of giving and receiving. How's your perspective?

6 What kinds of gifts has your church given to those in need?

_____

_____

_____

_____

_____

7 How have Christians been generous toward you?

_____

_____

_____

_____

_____

8 Why is stewardship a difficult area for many churches to deal with effectively?

_____

_____

_____

_____

_____

_____

9 What can you do to understand stewardship better and to evaluate your giving patterns?

RESPOND
to the message

_____

_____

_____

_____

_____

10 Why is it difficult for people to share their needs openly and honestly with fellow believers? Why is this attitude wrong?

_____

_____

_____

_____

_____

_____

11 What changes do you need to make in your giving habits?

RESOLVE
to take action

_____

_____

_____

_____

_____

A What does it mean to be content in every circumstance? How can we develop the ability to be more content?

MORE
for studying
other themes
in this section

B It seems inevitable that our circumstances will affect how we feel, think, and act. How did Paul rise above whatever was happening to him, whether good or bad?

C What can believers do to draw on the strength of Christ? What will he not help us do? What will he help you do that you never realized before?

D What kind of offering or sacrifice was Paul referring to in 4:18? What does this example suggest about God's response to Christian giving?

E Why does Paul refer to the other Christians around him as brothers and sisters? What does this tell us about the nature of the church?

LESSON 8
BACK TO THE BASICS
COLOSSIANS 1:1-14

REFLECT
on your life

1 Think of a sport and list its fundamentals.

_____

_____

_____

_____

_____

_____

2 Why is it important for athletes to master the fundamentals of their sport?

_____

_____

_____

_____

_____

READ
the passage

Read the introductory material to Colossians, Colossians 1:1-14, and the following notes:

❒ 1:1 ❒ 1:2, 3 ❒ 1:4, 5 ❒ 1:6 ❒ 1:8 ❒ 1:9-14 ❒ 1:12-14 ❒ 1:13

3 What roles do faith, hope, and love play in building a firm foundation for the Christian life?

_____

_____

_____

_____

4 What is the difference between learning to "know God better and better" (1:10) and increasing our knowledge about God?

_____

_____

_____

_____

Paul had never met the believers in Colosse, yet he felt burdened to pray for them and comfortable enough to encourage and teach them. The Colossian believers were very fortunate that Paul saw how they were being misled and then offered them the loving correction they needed. Paul cared enough about these brothers and sisters in Christ to challenge them and to help them get back to the basics. It's easy to become distracted from what is truly important in life and then drift even further from it. Where have you become distracted, or even been misled, as you follow Christ? Get back to the basics.

REALIZE
the principle

5 Why is it so important that believers agree about the fundamentals of the faith?

_____

_____

_____

_____

_____

6 How can churches prevent people from drifting away from a true understanding of the gospel?

RESPOND
to the message

_____

_____

_____

_____

7 Who or what has helped you avoid error in your doctrine?

_____

_____

_____

_____

8 How can you build a solid foundation for your faith?

_____

_____

_____

_____

_____

_____

9 What pressures or forces do you face that might confuse your understanding of Christian doctrine?

_____

_____

_____

_____

_____

_____

10 Where do you need help in sticking to the basics?

_____

_____

_____

_____

_____

_____

RESOLVE
to take action

11 What people, programs, books, or other resources can help answer your questions about your faith and keep you on the right track? What resource should you use right away?

_____

_____

_____

_____

_____

A Why did Paul write this letter to the Colossians? What kind of letter would he write to your church?

MORE
for studying
other themes
in this section

B What were some of the distinguishing features of the heresy at Colosse? How do each of the Megathemes serve as corrections to these? How are contemporary understandings of "spirituality" (as in the New Age movement) similar to and different from the Colossian heresy?

C Where else in the Bible does Paul emphasize the importance of faith, hope, and love as key elements of Christian experience? How are faith, hope, and love interrelated?

D What were the requirements for being an apostle? What was special about Paul's qualification? What special role does God have for you?

E What does it mean that God has "enabled" us to be a part of his Kingdom (1:12)? What is the inheritance in which we are allowed to share?

F How is the pattern of Paul's prayer in 1:9-14 similar to that of the Lord's Prayer? How does it differ? Compare Paul's prayer with your prayers for other Christians.

G What makes it difficult to live out the gospel? How does Paul's prayer encourage you to overcome these difficulties?

LESSON 9
THE WHOLE TRUTH AND
NOTHING BUT THE TRUTH
COLOSSIANS 1:15–2:5

1 Who has been quoted out of context in the news recently?

_____

_____

_____

2 How do people twist the truth without telling outright lies?

_____

_____

_____

_____

Read Colossians 1:15–2:5, the charts "The Colossian Heresy" and "Salvation through Faith," and the following notes:

❐ 1:15, 16   ❐ 1:15-23   ❐ 1:20   ❐ 1:21, 22   ❐ 1:22, 23   ❐ 1:24

❐ 1:28, 29   ❐ 2:4ff

3 What does 1:15-23 tell about the person and work of Jesus Christ?

_____

_____

_____

_____

4 What does 1:24–2:5 say about the role and responsibility of all believers?

_____

_____

_____

_____

5 Review the chart "The Colossian Heresy." How could such a distorted view of the gospel be attractive to people? Why was it so harmful for the believers?

_____

_____

_____

_____

_____

6 Why are people often tempted to add to the simple truth of the gospel?

_____

_____

_____

_____

_____

REALIZE
the principle

An insidious heresy was plaguing the church in Colosse—it added a deeper or special knowledge to the gospel. Paul refutes this heresy and urges the Colossians to trust in Christ alone. Whenever we add anything to the gospel, or take anything away, the effect is the same—we diminish Christ. By adding requirements for salvation, or less important doctrines, or any other element of man-made religion, we imply that the work of Christ somehow falls short of what people need to be reconciled to God. All we need is Christ! Make sure that you understand this and that you communicate it clearly when sharing your faith with others.

7 What are some modern distortions of the gospel message?

_____

_____

_____

_____

8 What might some people like to remove from the gospel? What might some like to add to the gospel?

_____

_____

_____

_____

_____

RESPOND
to the message

9 What can you do to protect yourself from distortions of the gospel?

_____

_____

_____

_____

10 Why is it so hard to accept the fact that we can do nothing to earn our salvation?

_____

_____

_____

_____

11 What would you tell someone who sincerely wanted to become a Christian?

_____

_____

_____

_____

12 Why is it important to communicate the gospel clearly?

_____

_____

_____

_____

13 Whom do you know who needs a clear presentation of the gospel? What first step can you take to tell that person about Christ?

RESOLVE
to take action

_____

_____

_____

_____

_____

_____

A Why does Paul say so little about the human attributes of Christ? What essential human qualities are presented?

MORE
for studying
other themes
in this section

B Why is the gospel a mystery to some people? Why might some Christians want to keep this sense of mystery about it?

C What do you think Paul meant in complimenting the Colossian church for "living as [they] should" (2:5)?

D How does truth encourage and unite believers?

E Why do many Christians often feel uncomfortable about sharing their faith? What can be done to overcome these uncomfortable feelings?

LESSON 10
SEARCHING FOR FULLNESS
COLOSSIANS 2:6-23

1 Describe a time when you were cheated in a purchase (e.g., what you bought was not as advertised).

_____

_____

_____

_____

_____

2 Describe a time when you almost got rid of something of high quality or of special value to you and then were glad that you decided to hang on to it.

_____

_____

_____

_____

Read Colossians 2:6-23 and the following notes:

❐ 2:6, 7   ❐ 2:7   ❐ 2:8   ❐ 2:10   ❐ 2:11, 12   ❐ 2:13-15   ❐ 2:15   ❐ 2:16, 17
❐ 2:19   ❐ 2:20-23   ❐ 2:22, 23   ❐ 2:23

3 What did Paul mean when he said that Jesus "canceled the record" (2:14)?

_____

_____

_____

_____

4 What does this section teach about our connection to Christ?

_____

_____

_____

_____

_____

5 How were many of the believers being judged?

_____

_____

_____

_____

6 How do Christ's death and resurrection relate to the Jewish laws?

_____

_____

_____

_____

_____

7 What were some of the pressures on these early believers that could cause them to falter in their walk with Christ?

_____

_____

_____

_____

_____

REALIZE
the principle

Paul urged the Colossians to continue walking with Christ. They were never to exchange the fullness of Christ for hollow philosophy, human regulations, or approval from others. Why would any believer in Christ want to make this kind of trade? In the church in Colosse there were those who were trying to lead believers away from Christ. Today, friends or co-workers may urge us to give up on Christ. Well-meaning religious people may want us to add some special regulations or interpretations of a doctrine to our simple faith. Don't allow anyone or anything to lead you astray. When you have Christ, you have all you need.

8 What are some of today's counterfeits of Christianity?

_____

_____

_____

_____

_____

9 What is legalism?

_____

_____

_____

_____

RESPOND
to the message

10 How does the gospel set us free from the tyranny of legalism?

_____

_____

_____

_____

11 Why are many Christians easily deceived or confused by false teaching?

_____

_____

_____

_____

12 What can a person do to become less vulnerable to false teaching? What can the church do to help?

_____

_____

_____

_____

13 In what areas are you susceptible to guilt coming from rules and regulations (legalism)?

_____

_____

_____

_____

_____

14 How can you develop strong roots in Christ? What resources are available to assist you in your growth?

RESOLVE
to take action

_____

_____

_____

_____

_____

A What was the purpose of circumcision? How is baptism related to circumcision?

MORE
for studying
other themes
in this section

B How did Christ triumph over the "spiritual rulers and authorities" (2:15)? What does his superiority mean for us?

C What does Paul mean in describing Christ as "the head of the body" (2:19)? Why was it especially important for the Colossian believers to understand and accept this idea fully?

D What does it mean to be free in Christ? What abuses of this freedom must we be careful to avoid?

LESSON 11
MAKING A CHANGE
COLOSSIANS 3:1-17

REFLECT
on your life

1 How have you broken a bad habit? How did others help you?

_____

_____

_____

_____

_____

READ
the passage

Read Colossians 3:1-17 and the following notes:

❐ 3:1ff ❐ 3:2, 3 ❐ 3:4 ❐ 3:8-10 ❐ 3:12-17 ❐ 3:14, 15 ❐ 3:16 ❐ 3:17

2 Why do you think Paul included particular sins in his list?

_____

_____

_____

_____

3 How is greed a form of idolatry?

_____

_____

_____

_____

_____

4 According to Paul, what is it that enables the believer to choose righteous behavior over sin?

_____

_____

_____

_____

_____

5 Paul urges us to "think about the things of heaven" (3:2). How does a Christian avoid being so heavenly minded as to be of no earthly good?

_____

_____

_____

_____

_____

REALIZE
the principle

6 If we have been "raised to new life with Christ," why do we still sin? Why is it so difficult to choose to do right?

_____

_____

_____

_____

_____

7 The note on 3:12-17 presents a strategy for effective Christian living. What practical steps can a person take to implement each suggested action?

_____

_____

_____

_____

_____

_____

Paul instructed the Colossians to put off the old life and put on the new. This summarizes how to live a life pleasing to God, but it doesn't happen easily or naturally. Putting to death our desires requires great struggle. Living a holy life is a ferocious battle against our earthly nature. But it is a battle with a strategy as simple as changing clothes—putting off the old and putting on the new. We may feel overwhelmed at times, but we never have to feel outmaneuvered. When you find a bad habit difficult to break, or when your thought life seems out of control, remember to set your mind and heart on God's priorities—and keep up the fight.

8 To what extent are the sins Paul listed still a problem in the church today? Why?

_____

_____

_____

_____

R
RESPOND
to the message

9 What happens when we serve God out of a sense of duty rather than out of genuine love? How can we avoid falling into this trap?

_____

_____

_____

_____

_____

10 What does 3:11-17 teach us regarding the purpose of fellowship, worship, and discipleship in the church?

_____

_____

_____

_____

_____

11 How should realizing that we are Christ's representatives affect our attitudes and actions?

_____

_____

_____

12 Identify some aspect of your behavior that has been difficult to change and is compromising your Christian life. What can you do to put this desire or habit to death? Who can support you?

RESOLVE
to take action

_____

_____

_____

_____

_____

A What does it mean that our life is now "hidden with Christ in God" (3:3)? How should that truth affect our life?

MORE
for studying
other themes
in this section

B What can believers expect from the coming wrath of God? What can nonbelievers expect?

C Paul stated that there were no divisions, distinctions, or differences between people in the church. How does your church reflect this truth? What are the implications for how you should treat other Christians?

D In this passage, Christians are referred to as God's chosen people. How do we qualify for this status that was first given to the Jews? What does it mean to be chosen by God?

E What is the "peace that comes from Christ" (3:15)? How does his peace relate to conflicts between believers?

LESSON 12
AT HOME AND ON THE JOB
COLOSSIANS 3:18–4:1

REFLECT
on your life

1 What is your favorite family-oriented TV show? How is it similar to real life? How is it different?

_____

_____

_____

_____

_____

_____

READ
the passage

Read Colossians 3:18–4:1, the chart "Rules of Submission," and the following notes:

❒ 3:18–4:1   ❒ 3:22–4:1

2 What are Paul's principles for building relationships?

_____

_____

_____

_____

_____

3 Why does Paul say that a wife's submission to her husband is "fitting for those who belong to the Lord" (3:18)?

_____

_____

_____

4 How might parents aggravate their children?

_____

_____

_____

_____

_____

_____

5 Regardless of our occupations or working conditions, we are still working for the Lord. How can a person work as though for the Lord and not people?

_____

_____

_____

_____

_____

_____

6 What are some common misconceptions about submission in marriage? Why do people get hung up on this command?

REALIZE
the principle

_____

_____

_____

_____

_____

_____

7 How can we train our children in the Lord?

_____

_____

_____

_____

_____

8 How should a Christian's attitude toward work differ from that of a non-Christian?

_____

_____

_____

_____

9 Why is it so difficult to put the needs of others first, even in close relationships?

_____

_____

_____

_____

Paul gives guidelines for relationships and attitudes toward family members and fellow workers. Often it's very difficult to live for Christ around our families and at work. This is where we are under the most pressure, where we spend most of our time, and where others come to know us best (and see us at our worst). The key to being Christlike wherever we are is looking out for the other person's best interests. Let your faith make a difference where it counts most—at home and on the job.

RESPOND
to the message

10 Describe an occasion in your marriage, home, work, or church where you chose to be submissive to someone when you didn't feel like it.

_____

_____

_____

_____

_____

11 What might you do to be more consistently Christlike in that area?

_____

_____

_____

_____

12 How can you express appreciation to your spouse, your children, and your co-workers this week for the contribution that each makes to your life?

_____

_____

_____

_____

RESOLVE
to take action

A Why is honoring one's parents so important that it was included as one of the Ten Commandments? What does _honoring_ involve? What can you do to honor your parents more?

B What should be your attitude toward your boss or another authority over you? How might this attitude affect your work?

MORE
for studying
other themes
in this section

LESSON 13
BUILDING RELATIONSHIPS IN THE BODY
COLOSSIANS 4:2-18

REFLECT
on your life

1 Imagine that you are putting together a team to accomplish a goal (sports, business, church, etc.). Explain the criteria you would use for choosing your team members.

_____

_____

_____

_____

_____

_____

2 How is the church like a team?

_____

_____

_____

_____

READ
the passage

Read Colossians 4:2-18 and the following notes:

❐ 4:2   ❐ 4:6   ❐ 4:7   ❐ 4:10   ❐ 4:12   ❐ 4:14   ❐ 4:15   ❐ 4:18

3 List all of the various forms of personal support and encouragement given in this passage.

_____

_____

_____

_____

_____

4 What do the people whom Paul mentions in his closing remarks have in
common besides their faith in Jesus Christ?

_____

_____

_____

_____

Paul ended his letter by giving final instructions to the church and sending his
greetings to others. This showed how much Paul valued relationships in the
church. Some of those mentioned were Paul's fellow workers, people with whom
he had served side by side. There is something unique about our relationships
with our fellow workers. They should be so genuine and honest that others are
attracted to us. Many people long to have those kinds of relationships. Who are
your fellow workers? How do you treat them?

REALIZE
the principle

5 What should characterize our relationships with other believers?

_____

_____

_____

_____

_____

6 Why is intercessory prayer such an important part of church life?

_____

_____

_____

_____

_____

RESPOND
to the message

7 Why should we challenge our fellow believers to attempt even more for
the Lord?

_____

_____

_____

_____

_____

8 How does your church support and encourage its members? its ministry staff and missionaries? What improvements would you like to see?

_____

_____

_____

_____

_____

_____

9 Who has been the greatest encouragement in your growth as a Christian? What did he or she do?

_____

_____

_____

_____

_____

RESOLVE
to take action

10 Identify at least one believer who could benefit from your prayers and encouragement this week. Pray for that person; then phone, write, visit, or find another tangible way to demonstrate your concern.

_____

_____

MORE
for studying
other themes
in this section

A Christians know that prayer is important, and yet many have an inconsistent or unsatisfying prayer life. What prevents us from praying more effectively? How can we improve?

B What do we learn about the nature of prayer in 4:2-4 and 4:12?

C What do you think Paul meant by his instruction to "make the most of every opportunity" (4:5) in our contact with non-Christians? What about the suggestion to "live wisely" (4:5)?

D Paul refers to Mark rather warmly in 4:10. Yet his relationship with Mark hadn't always been positive. What do you think happened to improve their relationship? What lesson can we learn from this?

E What effect would Paul's request to "remember my chains" (4:18) likely have had on the recipients of this letter? How could they remember Paul's chains? What Christians are in chains today? How can we remember them?

Take Your Bible Study
to the Next Level

The **Life Application Study Bible** helps you apply truths in God's Word to everyday life. It's packed with nearly 10,000 notes and features that make it today's #1–selling study Bible.

Life Application Notes: Thousands of Life Application notes help explain God's Word and challenge you to apply the truth of Scripture to your life.

Personality Profiles: You can benefit from the life experiences of over a hundred Bible figures.

Book Introductions: These provide vital statistics, an overview, and a timeline to help you quickly understand the message of each book.

Maps: Over 200 maps next to the Bible text highlight important Bible places and events.

Christian Worker's Resource: Enhance your ministry effectiveness with this practical supplement.

Charts: Over 260 charts help explain difficult concepts and relationships.

Harmony of the Gospels: Using a unique numbering system, the events from all four Gospels are harmonized into one chronological account.

Daily Reading Plan: This reading plan is your guide to reading through the entire Bible in one unforgettable year.

Topical Index: A master index provides instant access to Bible passages and features that address the topics on your mind.

Dictionary/Concordance: With entries for many of the important words in the Bible, this is an excellent starting place for studying the Bible text.

Available in the New Living Translation, New International Version, King James Version, and New King James Version. Take an interactive tour of the *Life Application Study Bible* at
www.NewLivingTranslation.com/LASB

CP0271